W9-DEU-757

LAS VEGAS

AT NIGHT

TRAM STATION
TO
MANDALAY
BAY
LUXOR

LAS VEGAS
AT NIGHT

Benjamin Marcus

PHOTOGRAPHY BY
Jason Hawkes & Karl Mondon

THUNDER BAY
P·R·E·S·S
San Diego, California

Thunder Bay Press
An imprint of the Baker & Taylor Publishing Group
10350 Barnes Canyon Road, San Diego, CA 92121
www.thunderbaybooks.com

Produced by Salamander Books,
an imprint of Anova Books Ltd.
10 Southcombe Street, London W14 0RA, UK

All notations of errors or omissions should be addressed to Thunder Bay Press, Editorial Department, at the above address. All other correspondence (author inquiries, permissions) concerning the content of this book should be addressed to Salamander Books, 10 Southcombe Street, London W14 0RA, UK.

Library of Congress Cataloging-in-Publication Data

Marcus, Benjamin.
Las Vegas at night / Benjamin Marcus.
p. cm.
ISBN-13: 978-1-60710-011-9
ISBN-10: 1-60710-011-8
1. Las Vegas (Nev.)--Pictorial works. 2. Las Vegas (Nev.)--Buildings, structures, etc.--Pictorial works. 3. Night--Pictorial works. 4. Night photography--Nevada--Las Vegas. I. Title.
F849.L35T47 2009
917.93'13500222--dc22

2009022223

1 2 3 4 5 13 12 11 10 09

Color Reproduction by Dot Gradations, Wickford, Essex, UK
Printed in China by 1010

CONTENTS

INTRODUCTION

New York may be the city that never sleeps, but Las Vegas is the city that truly comes alive at night. From the changing colored facades of the Rio casino to the spectacular displays on Fremont Street and the red neon spike topping the Stratosphere Tower, Las Vegas buzzes with neon energy.

A tour around Vegas is a visual treat to the eye. Mixed in with the vintage neon signs of Circus Circus and the Flamingo are architectural masterpieces from around the world. The Eiffel Tower jostles for attention with landmarks of old Venice while the Excalibur lights up its turrets and towers against the backdrop of the Sphinx and the Sky Beam emerging from Luxor's pyramid. Alongside these tributes to classic tourist destinations are casinos that have designed their own crowd-pulling shows: the erupting volcano of the Mirage, the sirens of Treasure Island (or "ti"), and the showstopping fountains of Bellagio.

Many books have captured the spectacular, ever-evolving street views of Las Vegas, but none have done so from the air. Until now, aerial views have been limited to those taken from the few high spots available, such as the top of the Eiffel Tower at the Paris Las Vegas, the Stratosphere Tower, or the roofs of the tallest hotels.

Las Vegas at Night adds some stunning vistas to the mix, all shot from a helicopter hovering high over the Strip. Jason Hawkes is one of the world's leading aerial photographers, with more than twenty books of aerial photography to his name. Hawkes has developed a complex twin-gyro camera stabilization system that allows him to take pin-sharp photographs with a shutter speed that evades the jarring motion of the helicopter's pounding rotors.

The sum total of this technology is a series of views of Las Vegas at night that have never been seen before, adding a dramatic new perspective to the city. Hawkes's images are complemented by specially commissioned ground views from San Francisco photographer Karl Mondon.

Having spent eighteen years shooting from helicopters and fixed-wing aircraft, Hawkes described his experience over Clark County as "the most frightening job I've ever worked on." With so many tourist helicopters in the air at any one time, he had to work with a spotter in the front seat; the spotter was specifically tasked with looking out for other helicopters. Their daring efforts resulted in the extraordinary images seen on these pages.

Ben Marcus

LAS VEGAS: A HISTORY IN NEON

Below: *The Pioneer Club opened at 25 East Fremont Street in 1942. The casino's welcoming sign and mascot is the iconic Vegas Vic. The forty-foot-tall version of Vic went up in 1951, complete with moving arm, cigarette, and a recording of his greeting—"Howdy, pardner!"—which went off every fifteen minutes.*

WATER FLOWING UNDERGROUND

In the beginning, there was water in the desert. And appropriately, the modern city of Las Vegas began with a huge gamble that paid off.

In 1829 an eighteen-year-old scout named Rafael Rivera broke off from an expedition led by Antonio Armijo. While Armijo was blazing a trade route from Santa Fe, New Mexico, to Mission San Gabriel in California, Rivera made a side bet, risking death by starvation, disease, thirst, hostile Native Americans, heat, cold, or just plain getting lost looking for easier passage, water, food—whatever was out there in the middle of the desert. Rivera broke off from the main group on Christmas day, and wasn't seen again for two weeks. What he found in between was as good as gold: a vast desert valley where water bubbled up from the ground—an oasis of running water and green trees. The area Rivera found was marked on maps as "Vegas," meaning "meadows."

Fifteen years later, in May 1844, John C. Frémont passed through the area during an expedition for the U.S. Topographical Corps. In his report, he wrote: "We encamped in the midst of another very large basin, at a camping ground called Las Vegas . . . Two narrow streams of clear water, four or five feet deep, gush suddenly with a quick current, from two singularly large springs . . . The taste of the water is good, but rather too warm . . . They, however, afford a delightful bathing place."

THERE WILL BE A RAILROAD

Eight years after the Mormons arrived in Salt Lake City, an expedition of thirty missionaries led by William Bringhurst constructed the first of Las Vegas's ambitious structures: an adobe fort, 150 feet square. The fort was built in 1855 on Las Vegas Creek, but heat and loneliness drove the Mormons back to Salt Lake City, and Las Vegas became a mostly abandoned outpost on "the Mormon Corridor" between Salt Lake City and Los Angeles.

President James Buchanan made Nevada a territory in 1861. Statehood came in 1865. Into the 1890s, ongoing rumors of a planned railway line through Las Vegas proved true when Montana senator William Clark surveyed the Las Vegas Valley as part of the route for his San Pedro, Los Angeles, and Salt Lake City Railroad.

Clark's railroad opened in January 1905. The 700-mile trip from Los Angeles to Salt Lake City—which used to take days and weeks of hard travel through merciless desert—now took exactly one day. Las Vegas had water, and Clark had ambitions for the place as an important train hub for the main line and also shorter routes into other parts of southern Nevada. On May 15, 1905, Clark auctioned 110 acres of property for an area he called the Clark Las Vegas Townsite, which is now Main Street north of Fremont Street.

William Clark was an opportunist and an enterprising scoundrel who died at the age of eighty-six as one of the fifty richest men in U.S. history at the time. Clark County was named in his honor in 1908.

CITY OF LAS VEGAS

Gambling had been illegal in Nevada for almost a year when Las Vegas officially became incorporated as a city on March 6, 1911. Prior to the new conservatism of 1910, gambling in Nevada had been legal since 1869, but in Las Vegas, those activities were limited to an area known as blocks 16 and 17. The plot of land that is now a parking garage behind the Golden Nugget and Binion's Horseshoe was Las Vegas's red-light district—the original Sin City—where alcohol, prostitution, and gambling defied the law.

After 1910, gambling was illegal in Nevada, and then by 1918 alcohol was illegal everywhere, but as the population of Las Vegas grew from 1,500 in 1911, to 2,304 in 1920, to 5,156 in 1930, the city became known as a haven of drinking, gambling, and other sins against the county, the state, the nation, and whatever gods you brought along.

DEPRESSION? WHAT DEPRESSION?

The stock-market crash of 1929 and ensuing Depression of the 1930s were good for Las Vegas. President Calvin Coolidge approved the Boulder Canyon Project on December 21, 1928, and the economic crisis sped the dam-building project as an opportunity to create jobs. By 1929, thousands of workers flowed in to lay a foundation for the dam and to build Boulder City—a federal town that disallowed alcohol, drugs, gambling, membership in unions, and any other sins that cut down on productivity. To this day, Boulder City is one of two places in Nevada where gambling is illegal.

Some Boulder City citizens snuck off to Las Vegas during their rare off-hours, and that flow was increased by Highway 91, built in 1929 to provide easier access for workers, tourists, and materials coming from California.

The contract to build the Boulder Dam was awarded to a consortium called Six Companies Inc. on March 11, 1931. Nine days later, "wide-open gambling" was made legal throughout Nevada. On April Fool's Day, the Clark County Commission granted its first four gambling licenses. The very first went to Mayme V. Stocker and J. H. Morgan, who paid $1,410 to operate a "Gambling and Slot Machine (2) business" for three months.

In 1931 a convicted California bootlegger named Tony Cornero and his two brothers built the Meadows on the corner of Fremont Street and Charleston Boulevard—one of the first legal casinos of the wide-open gambling era.

PEOPLE WILL COME

Prohibition was repealed in 1933, and the following year the chamber of commerce initiated "Helldorado Days," which framed Las Vegas as an Old West town with frontier roots where anything went: drinking, gambling, fighting—although they probably drew the line at firing six-shooters.

By 1939 the population was only 8,000 permanent residents. That number was multiplied by World War II, as the Basic Magnesium plant (in what is now Henderson) produced five million pounds of the lightweight metal each day for airplane wings. Northeast of town, the Army Air Corps' gunnery school (now Nellis Air Force Base) graduated 4,000 B17 and B29 gunners a week.

Below: *The Fremont Street Experience, circa 1931. The Overland Hotel showed the first moving picture in 1911. Fremont Street was paved in 1925. The Northern Club opened in 1912 and was granted the first gaming license in 1931—when "wide-open gambling" was made legal again. This view was taken from about where the Plaza Hotel is today.*

Right: *By 1932 the Apache Hotel on Fremont Street had the first neon sign in Las Vegas, and it was also the first Las Vegas hotel with air-conditioning and an elevator. The Golden Nugget opened in 1946, and by 1950, when Benny Binion opened the Horseshoe casino, neon was all the rage and the competing signs transformed Fremont Street into "Glitter Gulch."*

Far right: *In 1934 the Las Vegas Chamber of Commerce dreamed up "Helldorado Days"—a week of parades, rodeos, country and western dancing, beauty contests, eating, drinking, and making merry dressed as cowboys, miners, and other characters from Las Vegas's past. Helldorado Days ran from 1934 until 1998, then was revived to celebrate Las Vegas's centennial in 2005.*

There was an even larger population of defense workers a couple of hundred miles away in Southern California. Better roads, better automobiles, and wartime prosperity made Las Vegas accessible for weekend trips.

Liberace began a thirty-year run in Las Vegas in November 1944, and a year later, more than 12,000 soldiers and workers who had come to the desert decided to stay.

SWIMMING POOLS AND MOVIE STARS

After the war, Thomas Hull's El Rancho Hotel was an upward evolution in comfort and class, with a swimming pool, air-conditioning, buffets, and live entertainment from the biggest names. Hull located the El Rancho Vegas on Highway 91 and established what would become the Strip.

Benjamin "Bugsy" Siegel tried to buy the El Rancho Vegas but failed, so he partnered with Hollywood businessman Billy Wilkerson to build a more elaborate, classier joint. By March 1947, the Flamingo—which featured in the 1994 film *Bugsy*—was a hit. But Siegel himself was hit a few months later in Los Angeles. The murder and gruesome photos of Siegel made headlines and Sin City added new immoralities to its inventory: murder and organized crime.

THE HEAT

The population of Clark County was more than 48,000 by 1950, and there were sixteen daily flights into Las Vegas. A new kind of heat was focused on Las Vegas by the federal government, which made it part of a nationwide investigation into organized crime.

In 1951 the first aboveground nuclear test occurred at the Nevada Proving Grounds. The mushroom clouds rose for the next twelve years, and Las Vegas capitalized on the free fireworks show. In 1956 a twenty-one-year-old Elvis Presley performed in the Venus Room at the New Frontier Hotel, billed as "the Atomic Powered Singer."

Despite the heat and because of the heat, the 1950s saw a real-estate boom that produced a second generation of increasingly large, luxurious hotel/resort/casinos. The 225-room Desert Inn opened in 1950, followed a year later by the Sahara Hotel and the Sands Hotel.

THE DAWN OF THE RAT PACK

In September 1951, a somewhat down-on-his-luck Frank Sinatra first performed in Las Vegas, at the Desert Inn. In 1954 Ronald Reagan put on a two-week show at the Last Frontier, and by 1955 Liberace was the highest-paid entertainer in Las Vegas, earning $50,000 a week—the equivalent of $350,000 a week in today's money.

Las Vegas went segregated in 1955 with the opening of Joe Louis's Moulin Rouge casino, which allowed African Americans to work and stay as guests. And in 1955 the Strip went high-rise with the opening of the Riviera Hotel, which soared to nine stories and had 290 rooms. From the top of the Riviera, guests—and competing hotel owners—watched the Royal Nevada, Dunes, and Hacienda open in 1955, and the Tropicana and Stardust in 1958.

In 1957 the Dunes turned the heat up again when they brought the topless Minsky's Follies to the Strip. In 1958 the Stardust did that one better by bringing the first big show to the Strip: the Lido de Paris. In 1959 the Tropicana Hotel bought the American rights to the Folies Bergere. That same year, another name associated with Las Vegas began a long run when Wayne Newton opened at the Fremont Hotel with brother Jerry and the Jets.

The businessmen of Las Vegas and the chamber of commerce were constantly looking to increase traffic, and they got help from the federal government when a Republican Congress rewrote the tax code to allow travel and entertaining as deductible expenses if they were related to the business of business—like a convention.

In 1959 the Las Vegas Convention Center's first building was a 6,300-seat, silver-domed meeting hall next to a 90,000-square-foot exhibit hall. Conventioneers now flowed into Las Vegas year-round, even in the middle of the week, and business was better than ever.

VIVA LAS VEGAS

The 1960s began with the El Rancho Vegas burning to the ground, making way for the new Vegas swept in by a rogues' gallery that included Frank Sinatra, Howard Hughes, Kirk Kerkorian, Jay Sarno, Evel Knievel, and Elvis Presley.

The 1960 release of *Ocean's Eleven*—a caper movie set in Las Vegas—christened Sinatra, Dean Martin, Sammy Davis Jr., Peter Lawford, and Joey Bishop as "the Rat Pack." But not all of the media attention focused on Las Vegas was so positive. *The Green Felt Jungle*, written in 1963 by Ovid

Above: *The El Cortez is still there, after more than sixty-five years. Built by Marion Hicks and J. C. Grayson, the El Cortez opened in 1941 as Las Vegas's first resort. The corner of Sixth and Fremont was considered too far out in the sticks, but the El Cortez attracted nonstop business, and that success drew the likes of Bugsy Siegel, Meyer Lansky, Gus Greenbaum, and Moe Sedway, who formed a syndicate to buy the property in 1945. The El Cortez is now the centerpiece of the Fremont East District, a 2007 redevelopment to put a fresh face on vintage Vegas. The original El Cortez sign is still glowing strong today.*

Demaris and Ed Reid, was a scathing exposure of organized crime in Las Vegas going back to the involvement of Bugsy Siegel, Meyer Lansky, and Lucky Luciano in the 1940s. This brave book introduced the civilian world to the "skim" and other techniques the underworld had for pulling money out of no-receipts Las Vegas and under the noses of the authorities.

However, Las Vegas's image problem got a boost in 1964 when Elvis Presley starred with Ann-Margaret in *Viva Las Vegas*—a musical romance that gave the growing city a glamour and a theme song that still resonates.

By 1965 the Stardust had expanded to a thousand rooms and started the "supermotel" era. In the same year, the Thunderbird added on the world's longest neon sign facade.

THE HUGHES CORPORATION

Howard Hughes was sixty-one years old and already an American legend when he came to Las Vegas in November 1966. Hughes was born rich and came to Las Vegas even richer, flush with $500 million from the sale of TWA—$3 billion in today's money. Hughes arrived on Thanksgiving Day on a private train car, and he was immediately taken to the Desert Inn, where he rented suites on the top floor. When Desert Inn manager Moe Dalitz asked the Hughes entourage to vacate, Hughes offered to buy the hotel. When Dalitz asked for an inflated price of $13.2 million, Hughes paid it. Then Hughes bought KLAS Channel 8, the Sands, the New Frontier, Castaways, the unfinished Landmark, the Silver Slipper, and hundreds of thousands of square feet of commercial property.

Four years later, Hughes left Las Vegas. He died in 1976 without a will and his affairs took decades to straighten out, but Hughes's name and fame became attached to a city that had long been associated with mobsters.

CAESARS CIRCUS

Jay Sarno opened Caesars Palace in 1966: a European-style hotel that few thought would appeal to American tastes. Sarno and his partners went on to open their second casino, the family-friendly Circus Circus, in 1968, and they sold Caesars Palace in 1969 for $60 million. "Sarno took the town into another era," Steve Wynn was quoted by Rod Smith in the *Las Vegas Review Journal.*

In 1969 Kirk Kerkorian, a native of Fresno, California, of Armenian descent, began his rise to become Nevada's richest man when he opened the International Hotel on Paradise Road—where the Las Vegas Hilton is now. The International Hotel's 1,500 rooms made it the world's largest hotel, but Kerkorian went even bigger when he booked Barbra Streisand in the main showroom, the rock musical *Hair* in the other showroom, and Ike and Tina Turner in the lounge.

That worked, so Kerkorian made a deal with Elvis Presley to do a thirty-day run in the main showroom, replacing Streisand. For thirty days in a row, at $125,000 a week, Presley sold out the main showroom at the International, bringing incalculable goodwill, publicity, and profit to Kerkorian's new hotel—and to Las Vegas.

CASINOS AREN'T FOREVER

To get a taste for the 1970s, read *Fear and Loathing in Las Vegas: A Savage Journey to the Heart of the American Dream*. Hunter Thompson's drug-addled indictment of Las Vegas came out in 1971, the same year James Bond went to Las Vegas for *Diamonds Are Forever*—which spoofed the Howard Hughes legend in the form of Willard Whyte, a reclusive billionaire kidnapped by Ernest Blofeld and guarded by sexy bodyguards Thumper and Bambi.

In 1971 the Plaza opened downtown, and Circus Circus added a hotel to the casino in 1972. Steve Wynn was only thirty-one years old when he acquired the Golden Nugget in 1972, making him the youngest casino owner in history. In 1972 the Hilton Hotel Corporation bought the International Hotel, but Kerkorian had gone on to bigger things. He bought the Metro-Goldwyn-Mayer movie studios in 1969, and four years later built the world's largest hotel over the bones of the Bonanza Hotel. Kerkorian branded it the MGM Grand in honor of the movie *Grand Hotel*. The MGM Grand opened in 1973 with 2,100 rooms and was the largest in the world at the time.

By the late 1970s there were casinos dedicated to Rome, Hollywood, the Wild West, and the circus. Asian games had been popular in Las Vegas going back to cowboy days, but they didn't have a temple until the Imperial Palace opened on the Strip in 1979.

LONG STRING OF BAD LUCK

The 1970s were not the best years for Las Vegas, as can be gleaned from *Fear and Loathing*, *Diamonds Are Forever*, and Nicholas Pileggi's book *Casino*—which was adapted for the big screen in 1995. The names in *Casino* were changed to protect the innocent and guilty, but it's all based on the true story of a Jewish bookmaker and an Italian thug victimized by Las Vegas's transition from the 1970s into the 1980s.

The Monopoly board game is based on Atlantic City, New Jersey, and in 1976 Atlantic City ended Las Vegas's monopoly on casino gambling. Atlantic City didn't have "wide-open gambling" like Las Vegas, but the Resorts International opened in 1978 and by 1988 there were a dozen hotel/casinos open in Atlantic City, while there were no new major hotel/casinos on the Strip.

Howard Hughes died in 1976, followed by Elvis Presley in 1977. Sin City's bad luck continued in 1980, when a fire at the MGM Grand killed eighty-seven people. That was followed a year later by a fire at the Las Vegas Hilton in 1981 that killed eight people. In 1982 the U.S. Air Force's Thunderbirds were practicing out of Nellis Air Force Base. The leader had a malfunction and dove into the ground, with the rest of his team following him. All were killed.

PARTY UNTIL IT'S 1999

With all the planning, construction, and business happening on the East Coast, the gaming industry was distracted away from Las Vegas for more than a decade. Steve Wynn had been involved in the opening of the Golden Nugget in Atlantic City, but in the mid-1980s, Wynn turned his attention

Below: *The Golden Nugget proudly displays "1905" as the year Las Vegas became a railroad stop between Los Angeles and Salt Lake City. This version of the Golden Nugget was built in 1946 by Guy McAfee, a former vice detective from Los Angeles who must have decided that vice does pay. This photo was taken around 1959, when country music singer Bob Wills moved to Las Vegas to perform. The Golden Nugget was a "gambling hall" only until 1973, when Steve Wynn became president and added hotel rooms. When Wynn bought the place in 1973 at the age of thirty-one, he was the youngest casino owner in Las Vegas history.*

back to Las Vegas and the city began a new escalation that is still going today.

Financed with $600 million, the Mirage opened on the Strip in 1989. As the first "megaresort," it boasted over 3,000 rooms, an exploding volcano out front, and a jungle with waterfalls inside. The Mirage began an unprecedented run of construction along the Strip, which included the Excalibur (1990), Luxor (1993), MGM Grand (1993), Stratosphere (1996), New York–New York (1997), Bellagio (1998), Mandalay Bay (1999), and Venetian (1999).

THE ENTERTAINMENT CAPITAL OF THE WORLD

In 2001 Wynn took a breather, looked out over Las Vegas, and saw that it was good: "What I love the most about this town is the terrific opportunity it presents to those with the imagination and daring to build new must-see properties. Where else could you find a pyramid next to Camelot, next to the Statue of Liberty and Monte Carlo, an Italian lake next to the Roman Empire? Here this madness is okay. Anyplace else, they'd lock you up. The best is yet to come. The next five years will see a renaissance of entertainment here."

And that prediction, like many of the other calls Wynn has made, has proved true. Plug the words "the entertainment capital of the world" into any Internet search engine, and one of the first things you'll see is "Las Vegas."

In the past, Louis Prima in the lounge, the Rat Pack in the nightclub, and dancing girls in the showroom were sideshows to the main event: entertainment was a shill to lure guests into the casinos, where the real money was. But in the twenty-first century, Minsky's Follies, the Folies Bergere, and Lido de Paris of the 1950s have been replaced by Bite, Sin City Bad Girls, and Thunder from Down Under.

Instead of Ol' Blue Eyes, it's the Blue Man Group. Liberace is gone, but Elton John has taken his place. The Beatles played Las Vegas in 1964, and the city remembers them with LOVE, a Beatles tribute at the Mirage.

Where movie stars and Olympic swimmers used to perform swan dives from high boards, now Las Vegas has spectacular water shows like Le Rêve and O.

At any time, Las Vegas has dozens of magic shows, production shows, adult shows, comedy shows, tribute shows, hypnosis shows, and afternoon shows for the kids.

Entertainment has been Vegasized, turning magicians into rock stars, and giving musicians—from Donny and Marie

Left: *"Glitter Gulch" is a Wild West expression going back to the nineteenth century—a synonym for "red-light district" and "the line"—to denote the wild side of town where a cowboy could find alcohol, gambling, prizefighting rings, and women of easy virtue. Fremont Street took on the name of Glitter Gulch in the 1940s, because that is where a cowboy could find all those activities but also because of the explosion of neon signs. At one time, Sassy Sally's was a burlesque club called Reed's Cabaret, but when that fell out of fashion, it turned into the Sassy Sally slots casino.*

Far left: *The Landmark Hotel operated from 1969 to 1990, and became a landmark for struggling Las Vegas dreams. Kansas City building contractor Frank Carroll borrowed $3 million and bought property off the Strip to build a hotel inspired by Hollywood's Landmark Hotel as well as the Seattle Space Needle. Originally fifteen stories, the Landmark got into a "space race" with the Mint Hotel and shot for thirty-one stories. The teamsters loaned him $6 million, but that still wasn't enough, and Howard Hughes bought the unopened hotel for $17 million as part of his buying spree in 1968. When Hughes signed the Landmark over to ex-wife Jean Peters in their divorce agreement, he wasn't being giving. The Landmark changed hands through the 1970s and 1980s, closed in 1990, and was imploded in 1995 with the interior lights on—as seen in the movie* Mars Attacks!

to Prince—their choice of dozens of venues, large and small, to rock the town for a day or a couple of months.

Gaming is now a part of the total entertainment package, which draws forty million visitors to Las Vegas every year. They fill an inventory of hotel rooms that was 130,000 at the last count but is growing daily with every floor of a new or remodeled hotel.

In 2006 the *Las Vegas Sun* produced an elaborate review and overview of Las Vegas called "Boomtown: The Story Behind Sin City." The report included this summary: "Today Las Vegas is home to two million people. Each month, 6,000 residents settle in the Clark County area, making Las Vegas one of the fastest-growing cities in the nation. Vegas is also the number-one destination spot in the world, passing the theme park draw of Orlando, Florida, in 1999, and the spiritual pull of Mecca in 2001. In 2006 Las Vegas drew in an estimated forty million visitors. It boasted a total of over 130,000 hotel rooms, powered 15,000 miles of lighted neon tubing, housed more than 200,000 slot machines, and used over 222 million megawatt hours of electricity."

But that was 2006. Since then, the Palazzo opened, bringing another 3,042 hotel rooms, and Planet Hollywood took over from the Aladdin and is building the Planet Hollywood Towers, which will add another 1,200 luxury condos to the inventory.

And then there is CityCenter. This city-within-a-city will add as much as seventeen million square feet of hotel rooms, condominiums, retail, casinos, theaters, spas, and convention area to the middle of the Las Vegas Strip. CityCenter was originally projected to cost $4 billion, but that prediction had leapt to $11 billion as workers scurried to prepare the complex for an August 2009 opening. Ambitious? Insanely ambitious. To see the multiple high-rise towers of CityCenter going up before your eyes is to not believe your eyes. Las Vegas is building the equivalent of a modern downtown area in only a couple of years.

But that is Las Vegas: No plan is too audacious, no gamble too huge. Roll the dice. Try to find a route from New Mexico to California. Leave the main group for two weeks, and see what you can find.

WELCOME
TO Fabulous
LAS VEGAS
NEVADA
MANDALAY BAY
THEhotel

Left: *There are several "Welcome to Fabulous Las Vegas" signs located around the city—and even more copycats and replicas at a variety of businesses. But this sign, located south of town, is the original. The sign was designed by Betty Willis, a Las Vegas native who attended art school in Los Angeles, then came home to work as a commercial artist. In the mid-1950s, Willis designed the sign for the Moulin Rouge—the first segregated casino in Las Vegas. In 1952 a local neon sign store owner named Ted Rogich asked his designer, Willis, to make a distinctive sign welcoming everyone to the growing city. Willis placed the seven letters in "welcome" on silver dollars—for the Silver State. The final sign was twenty-five feet high and Rogich sold it to the city for $4,000 in 1959. The original sign has been moved farther south as the Strip has expanded, and there are similar signs located all around town, officially and unofficially. Willis and Rogich never patented the sign design, and it was their gift to their hometown.*

Right: *The stretch of road now known officially as State Route 604 and Las Vegas Boulevard—and unofficially as the Las Vegas Strip—had many names in the past: Fifth Street, the Arrowhead Highway, the Los Angeles Highway, and the Salt Lake Highway. Begun in the 1920s, Highway 91 originally ran 1,468 miles, from the Canadian border with Montana, to Long Beach, California. Highway 91 through town became known as State Route 604 in the 1970s, and Las Vegas Boulevard. Interstate 15 replaced most of Highway 91 in the 1970s. Mandalay Bay is the farthest point south on the Strip. This view looks to the southwest over the Luxor and Mandalay Bay. The road to the left is the Strip. The bright lights leading into the big city are those of cars on Interstate 15.*

Right: *The Strip, as seen from south to north, looking along the west side of Las Vegas Boulevard and off into the future. In 2006 the* Las Vegas Sun *produced an online documentary called "Boomtown: The Story Behind Sin City." The narration included these facts, as they were true in 2006: "Today Las Vegas is home to two million people. Each month, six thousand residents settle in the Clark County area, making Las Vegas one of the fastest-growing cities in the nation. Vegas is also the number-one destination spot in the world, passing the theme park draw of Orlando, Florida, in 1999, and the spiritual pull of Mecca in 2001. In 2006 Las Vegas drew in an estimated forty million visitors. It boasted a total of over 130,000 hotel rooms, powered 15,000 miles of lighted neon tubing, housed more than 200,000 slot machines, and used over 222 million megawatt hours of electricity."*

MANDALAY BAY

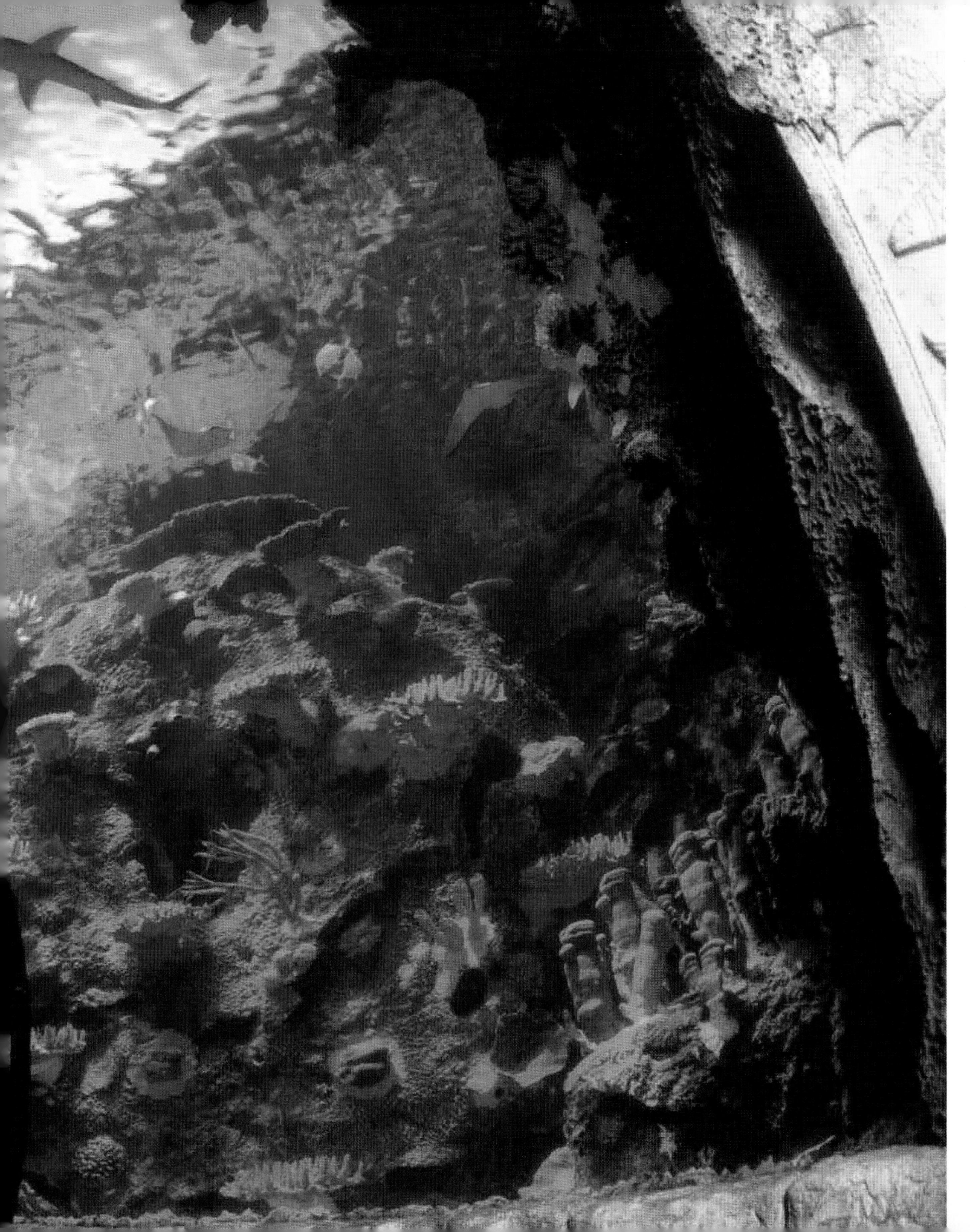

Left: *Shark Reef Aquarium at Mandalay Bay. Humans first appeared in the Las Vegas area 12,000 years ago, toward the end of the Pleistocene era, a time of global cooling and worldwide glaciation that began a million years before. Prior to that, for hundreds of millions of years, the Las Vegas area was underneath an ocean, where the ancestors of modern sharks and rays thrived:* Helicoprion *(spiral saw),* Scapanorhynchus *(spade snout), and* Stethacanthus, *which had a dorsal fin like an ironing board but apparently no clever nickname. Las Vegas was founded on water that bubbled up from the ground, and grew from the waters that powered steam trains and grew crops. From a trickle of humanity to a tsunami, now tens of millions of tourists visit each year because of the waters: in swimming pools and hot tubs, canals and wave pools, and also Mandalay Bay's Shark Reef Aquarium, which surrounds visitors in a cylinder of water and puts them face-to-face with sharks, rays, and other creatures that haven't been native to Las Vegas for millions of years.*

Right: *The Luxor Hotel is named for the Egyptian city on the Nile—formerly known as Thebes—that is one of the most important historical sites in the world. Oddly, there are no pyramids in Luxor, and the actual statue of the Sphinx is in Giza. The city of Luxor is considered the "world's greatest open-air museum," with massive buildings and a lot of statues. The Las Vegas Luxor took a few liberties with reality. The Luxor pyramid is thirty-six stories high, but shorter than the Great Pyramid of Giza to accommodate air traffic from McCarran Airport, which is a stone's throw to the east. The Sphinx at the Luxor Hotel is two stories taller than the original Sphinx—but it faces east, as opposed to the original west. Some say that repositioning the Sphinx has brought bad luck to the Luxor, but the hotel has been one of Las Vegas's most popular since it opened in 1993.*

Right: *Of the million points of light in Sin City, the Luxor Sky Beam is the most powerful of them all. Computer-designed mirrors focus thirty-nine xenon lamps into the strongest single beam of light on earth. The Luxor claims that you could read a newspaper by the beam ten miles up—and it's also clearly visible from outer space. Pilots can see the beam from as far as 250 miles away. At ground level, the beam is to night navigation what the Stratosphere Tower is to daytime navigation. If you can see the beam, you have some idea where in Las Vegas you are.*

Above: *Walk through like an Egyptian. The Luxor opened in 1993, the same year as Treasure Island and the new MGM Grand. Over the years, the Luxor has undergone extensive remodeling, moving away from the mysteries of 2100 BC to the pleasures of the twenty-first century. Instead of mummies, there is the "Bodies" exhibit. The RA nightclub closed and is now the LAX. It may be more modern, but the magic is still there, from Criss Angel's Cirque du Soleil production to the legendary restorative powers of being inside a giant pyramid.*

Right: *It may be strong enough to be seen from space, but flying critters like it, too. While the Luxor Sky Beam is close to McCarran Airport, neither NASA nor the FAA has acted against it. The beam is on the flight path for helicopter tours, which regularly fly through it. And like a giant camping lantern, the beam also attracts millions of insects, which in turn attract thousands of bats, all swirling and glinting in the light like confetti.*

MGM GRAND

Left: *The Excalibur is sixth-century Arthurian/British in theme, but the high walls, higher towers, and colored turrets are a riff on the fortified city of Carcassone in southeast France—which was begun by the Romans in 100 BC and then remodeled by the Visigoths, and then the French. Circus Circus Enterprises opened the hotel with 4,000 rooms in June 1990. It was the world's largest hotel and was of the "family-friendly" genre: entire floors dedicated to entertainment for underage guests, and a swimming pool designed for the whole family. And if a family loves medieval England, this is the place—the hotel has jousters, court jesters, the Roundtable Buffet, and the Steakhouse at Camelot.*

Above: *If Bavarian fantasy castle designer Mad King Ludwig—or perhaps Emperor Napoléon—came to Las Vegas, the allure of the Excalibur would capture them. And if Ludwig or Napoléon loved television, the Excalibur's 2,000 newly developed "Widescreen Rooms" have plasma screens fit for a king—or an emperor.*

Right: *"X" marks the MGM Grand: A Hollywood-themed super hotel/resort/casino that is a world unto itself. The main hotel building has 4,293 rooms, with 751 suites. Each of the three Signature at MGM Grand towers has 576 suites. The high rollers go for the fifty-one Skylofts, and the Mansion at MGM Grand offers even more exclusive accommodations with twenty-nine villas. Built on the bones of the Tropicana Country Club and the Marina Hotel, the MGM Grand was the second Strip hotel to have that name. It opened in December 1993 and gave the world a taste of "Maximum Vegas"—a lion cage, waterfalls, rivers, a CBS television studio, more than a dozen restaurants and bars, the Studio 54 and other nightclubs, a convention center, and the MGM Grand Adventures Theme Park for the whole family.*

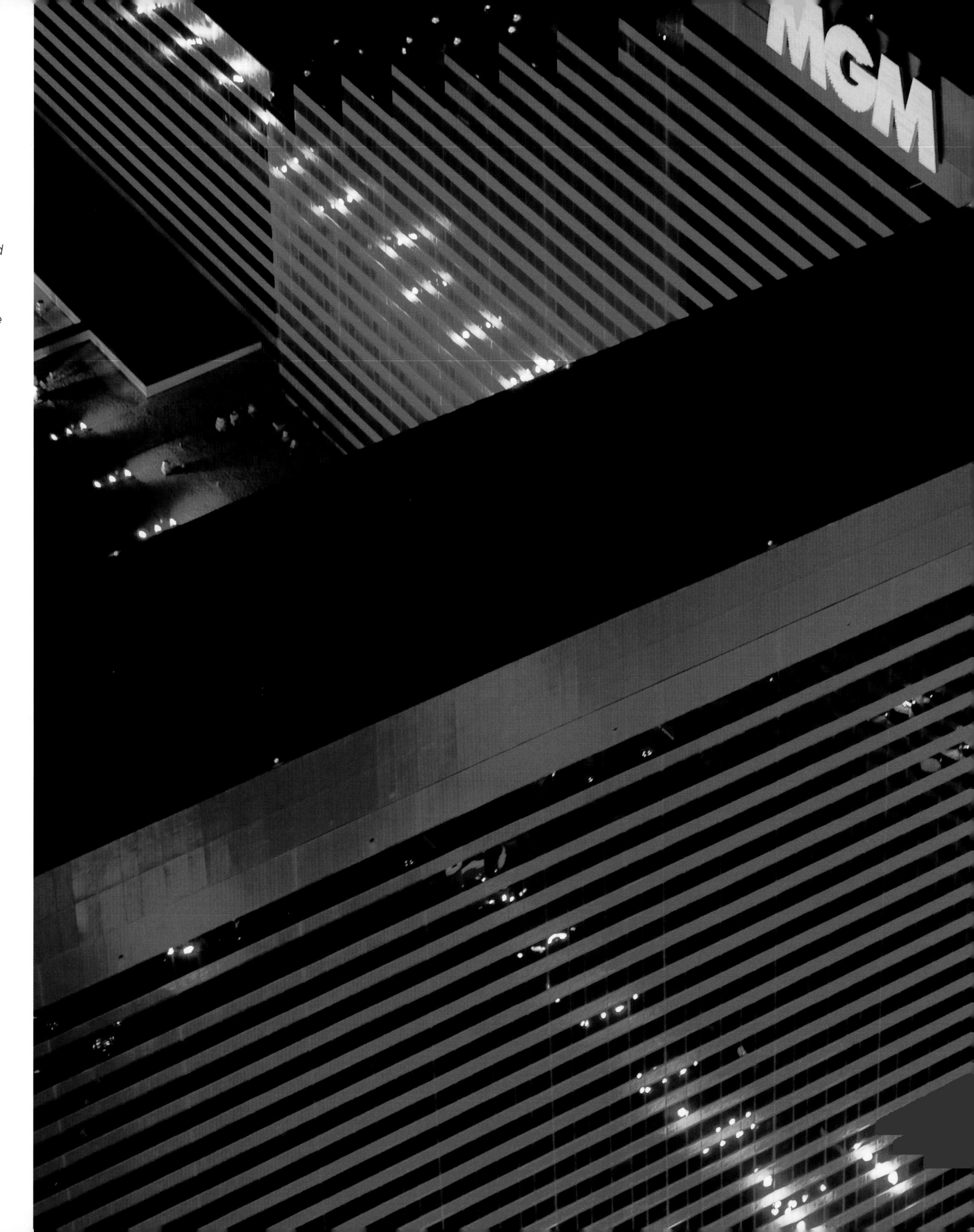

MGM
MGM GRAND

Above: *What once was is there no longer. The MGM Grand entrance was originally a Vegasized version of MGM mascot Leo the Lion: mouth open and roaring to allow guests into the casino and hotel. It was a good idea until MGM management wondered why all the Chinese guests were using another entrance—or not coming in at all. It turned out that in feng shui, walking into the mouth of a lion is considered bad luck. Chinese gamblers saw the open mouth of the lion and its fangs as an invitation to step inside and get eaten alive—financially—so they avoided the MGM Grand after it opened in 1993. Some Strip experts say that the Chinese New Year is the second-biggest gambling day of the year after the Super Bowl, and that made it worth the while of the MGM Grand's management to remove the inauspicious lion and replace it with another lion: a forty-five-foot-tall, 100,000-pound bronze sculpture of a proud lion—showing its chest but not its fangs.*

Right: *The MGM Grand is lined with a dozen of these pylons, all of them topped with statuary that riffs off the Oscar statue, without drawing the ire of the Academy. Looking for symbolism, these statues reflect the tireless effort of Las Vegas to keep its guests comfortable, entertained, and coming back.*

Below: *Nightclubs have been a part of Las Vegas going back to the earliest days, but you have to wonder what Frank and Sammy and Dean would think if they walked their drinks and cigarettes into Studio 54. This 22,000-square-foot pleasure palace has two levels and four dance floors, and was created in the image of the famous, celebrity-fueled New York nightclub of the 1970s and 1980s, from the black-and-white celebrity photos on the walls to the confetti and balloons falling on and around the dancers each night.*

Right: *New York City is so popular that they rebuilt it in 1997 on the corner of South Las Vegas Boulevard and West Tropicana. Where the island of Manhattan crams more than eight million people into nearly 470 square miles, New York–New York condenses 2,000 hotel rooms and a dozen familiar New York City landmarks into a single block of land along the Strip. A real New Yorker could tell you which building is which in the faux skyline: the Empire State Building, the Century Building, the Seagram's Building, the 55 Water Tower, the Lever House Soap Company, the Municipal Building, the AT&T Building, the Chrysler Building, the CBS Building, the New Yorker Hotel, the Liberty Plaza, and the Ziggurat Building. Strangely, the Twin Towers of the World Trade Center were not included in the original design. The interior is as Manhattanesque as the exterior. The 84,000-square-foot casino has a Central Park theme. For sports fans, the ESPN Zone has 165 television screens and there are another forty-five televisions and twelve big screens in the sports arena. For families, there is a Coney Island–style amusement area with bumper cars and Nathan's hot dogs. The Park Avenue area is for shopping and the Financial District is where you go to cash in chips—or buy more.*

Vdara
NEW YORK
NEW YORK
ZUMANITY
CIRQUE DU SOLEIL

Above: *The real thing opened May 1, 1931, and is 1,250 feet to the 102nd floor and then another 203 feet to the pinnacle. The Las Vegas replica is one-third the size of the original, forty-seven stories in a building topping out at 529 feet. That height doesn't make the top ten of Las Vegas's tallest buildings, which is headed by the Stratosphere Tower. At 1,149 feet, the Stratosphere is nearly as tall as the Empire State Building.*

Right: *The real Brooklyn Bridge is a mile long, eighty-five feet wide, and the towers are 277 feet above the water. The Las Vegas version is a 300-foot-long, fifty-foot-high bridge to nowhere crossed by fifteen million people a year. Like Manhattan, New York-New York is accessed by several bridges—one across Tropicana Way and another across South Las Vegas Boulevard—because the traffic at this corner of the Strip is as thick and dangerous as anything in Manhattan.*

Pepsi-Cola
NBA, COLLEGE BASKETBALL AND

NEW YORK
ZUMANITY
CIRQUE DU SOLEIL

Right: *The New York–New York roller coaster, formerly known as the Manhattan Express, is now known simply as the Roller Coaster. Some say the Roller Coaster is an authentic tribute to Coney Island, while others say it replicates the crazed thrill of a cab ride through Manhattan. The three-minute ride begins and ends within the casino, rising to 203 feet above the Strip and then dropping 144 feet, reaching a top speed of sixty-seven miles per hour before doing a 180-degree loop and an inverted, fighter-pilot twist and other dips and doodles before reentering the hotel. Recent economic turmoil has inspired some guests to refer to the Roller Coaster as "Wall Street" or "the Dow Jones."*

Following pages: *All roads lead to casinos in Las Vegas—especially the roads named for casinos. Built in 1957, the Tropicana Hotel gave its name to Tropicana Way, which bisects Las Vegas for sixteen miles from the Las Vegas Wash in the east to South Hualapai Way in the west. Along the way, Tropicana passes golf courses and McCarran Airport, as well as miles of urban sprawl, housing developments, and strip malls. Tropicana Way also forms a great divide between the Excalibur and the New York–New York. This view—hovering above the MGM Grand—looks west, with one wing of the Tropicana visible at the bottom left. The casino to the right of the New York–New York is the Monte Carlo.*

Monte Carlo

Monte Carlo
Monte Carlo

Left: *In the mid-1800s, Monaco was the poorest state in Europe. Prince Charles III made gambling legal in the 1850s, but it wasn't until a train line was laid and the Monte Carlo casino was completed in 1868 that gambling thrived. After only five years of casino gambling—and all that came with it—Monaco suspended income taxes. The principality thrived.*

Opening in June 1996, the Monte Carlo Las Vegas Hotel and Casino was built to bring the elegance and success of Monaco's Place du Casino to Las Vegas. The Monte Carlo's 3,002 hotel rooms and 259 luxury suites mean that Las Vegas's Monte Carlo has more guest rooms in fifty-five acres than Monaco has in all of its three-quarters of a square mile.

Above: *The official motto for Monaco—*Deo Juventa*—means "With God's help" in Latin. Variations on that motto are whispered or shouted in various forms around the gaming tables and slot machines of the Monte Carlo casino. This winged angel and entourage give their blessing to all who enter the Monte Carlo through the main arch.*

Left: *European-style hotel/casinos in Las Vegas go back to the opening of Caesars Palace in 1966. But the fascination with France goes back to the 1950s, when Las Vegas imported the Lido de Paris and Folies Bergere lock, stock, and garters from Paris. In 1999 the Paris Las Vegas opened with Catherine Deneuve flicking a switch to light up the replica Eiffel Tower and start a thunderous fireworks display from the top. A full-size, 1,063-foot Eiffel Tower was the original goal, but that plan was reduced to 460 feet by officials of the FAA and McCarran International Airport. Whether viewed from the ground looking up or from the observation deck looking down, the view is beautiful—especially at night.*

Right: *The Paris Las Vegas is a classy tribute to France's La Ville Lumière—the City of Lights. The lights of the Eiffel Tower, Fontaine des Mers, the Montgolfier balloon, the Arc de Triomphe, and the thirty-four-floor hotel illuminate the middle block of the Las Vegas Strip. At night, sitting outdoors at Mon Ami Gabi, eating pommes frittes, people-watching while serenaded by the Bellagio's musical fountain show across the street—that combination is one of the best effects of Las Vegas.*

TRUMP
TREASURE ISLAND
THE MIRAGE
THE MIRAGE
LOVE
THE MIRAGE
CASINO & RESORT
TERRY FATOR
CAESARS PALACE
CHER
Flamingo
BALLYS
hollywood
ph
BELLAGIO
O
planet hollywood
ph
MIRACLE MILE SHOPS

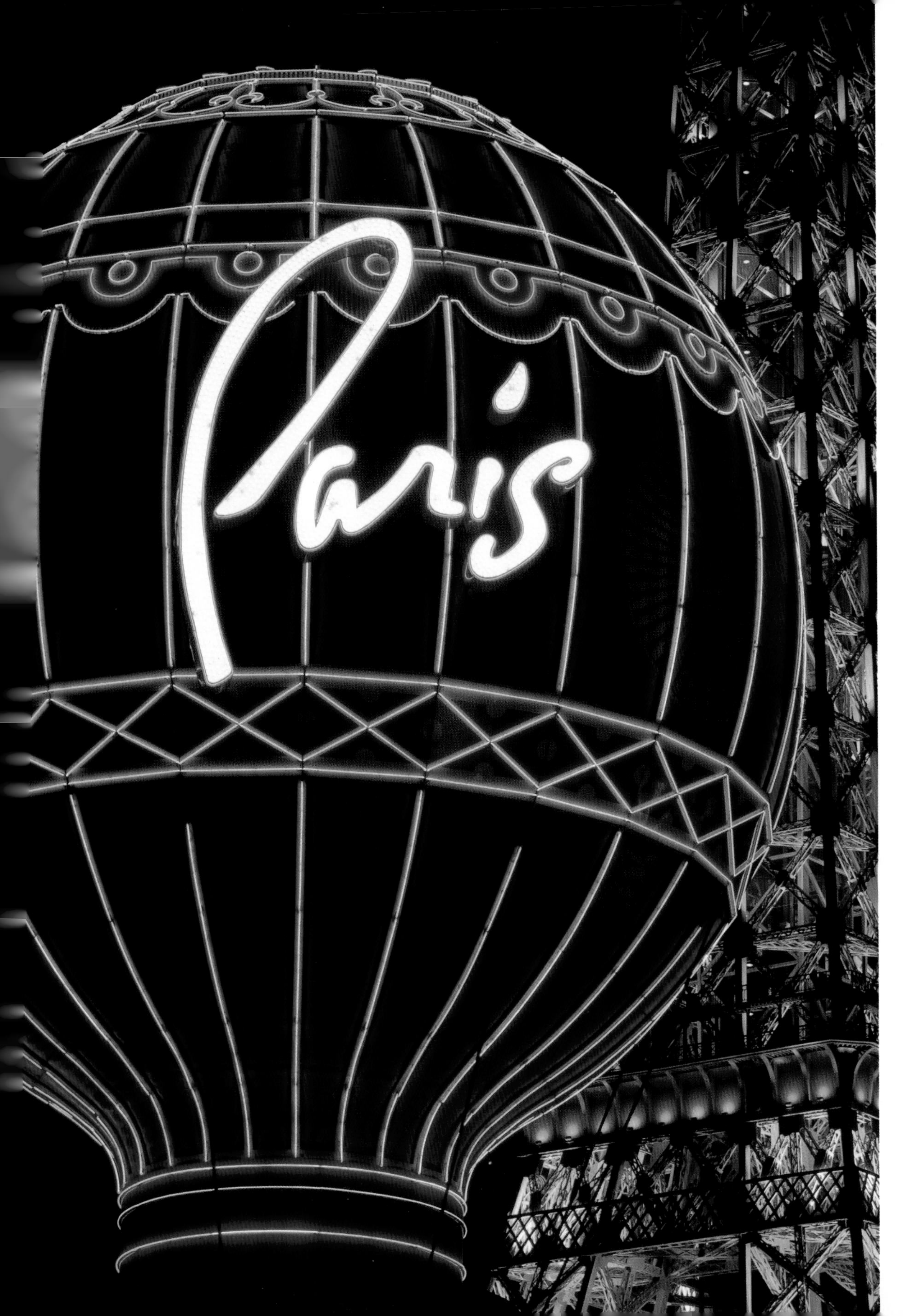

Left: *In 1783 the Montgolfier brothers felt confident enough in their experiments with unmanned hot-air craft to build a beautiful blue balloon decorated with the signs of the zodiac. The original Montgolfier balloon was seventy-five feet high and forty-six feet in diameter, and the 60,000 cubic feet of heated air trapped within lifted several daring humans as high as 3,000 feet over Paris. King Louis XVI made their father, Pierre, a member of the nobility and the French have been proud of that high-flying name ever since. That is the backstory to the beautiful blue-and-gold marquee for the Paris Las Vegas—a tribute to France, and man's first successful defeat of gravity.*

Right: *Before Napoléon took power in France and across Europe, there was a 1758 plan to build a giant elephant where the Arc de Triomphe now stands in Paris. Two and a half centuries later, it's probably good for Las Vegas's round-the-clock partygoers that they aren't confronted with a giant elephant after a hard night at the clubs. The original Arc de Triomphe was commissioned in 1806 to celebrate Emperor Napoléon's victory at Austerlitz. The final structure wasn't completed until the 1830s, and it now stands 162 feet high. The Paris Las Vegas version of the Arc de Triomphe is two-thirds the size of the original, but is detailed down to the names of the battles of the Napoleonic Wars, and the generals who fought them. Where the original stands over France's Tomb of the Unknown Soldier and the eternal flame, Las Vegas's Arc de Triomphe marks the entrance roundabout for the hotel/casino.*

Right: *Just across the way from the Paris Las Vegas, Planet Hollywood is one of the newest hotel/resort/casinos on the Strip. The hotel with 2,500-plus rooms took over a space from the Aladdin, a venerable hotel/casino that first opened in 1966. Elvis and Priscilla Presley were married there the following year. The Aladdin was imploded in 1998 and rebuilt and renovated over the next two years at a cost of $1.4 billion. The new Aladdin had an inauspicious beginning on August 17, 2000: problems with the fire inspector and the casino surveillance system caused a lockout of players and guests, and that caused customers to walk out on opening night. That hard opening stayed hard, as the new Aladdin couldn't find the old magic and declared bankruptcy a year later. Even by Las Vegas standards, the transition from Aladdin to Planet Hollywood was unusual: an expensively remodeled hotel closing in one year and then extensively remodeled again. Planet Hollywood teamed up with Bay Harbour Management and Starwood Hotels and Resorts Worldwide to buy the Aladdin in June 2003 for only $400 million. Over the next four years they invested $600 million to transform the Aladdin from medieval Arabia to modern Hollywood. During the transition, the hotel stayed open as the facade was stripped of its stone facing and moved several centuries forward to twenty-first-century electric signage that could probably be seen from space on its own. At one point, they started to paint the entire building blue, and made it up about fifteen floors before they decided the blue was no good, and painted it back to white. What did work in blue was the ceiling of the retail area formerly known as the Shops in Desert Passage. The cobblestones came off the floor and were replaced by black tile. The retail area was renamed the Miracle Mile—an endless corridor of shops and restaurants topped with an oddly soothing sky-blue ceiling that is a tribute to the Elvis song "Viva Las Vegas." By April 2007, any remnant of the Aladdin was gone and the remodeled Planet Hollywood Resort and Casino opened with Bruce Willis, Carmen Electra, Pete Sampras, Sugar Ray Leonard, and Roger Clemens bringing their celebrity power to the opening. And that has proven to be the magic.*

planet
ph
ph
BELLAGIO
O

Left: *Nowhere else on the Strip do two opposing hotels complement each other so well. The Bellagio was built by Steve Wynn's Mirage Resorts and opened in 1998. The Paris Las Vegas was opened by Park Place Entertainment in 1999 and is now owned by Harrah's. The Paris and Bellagio are hotels of the same vintage and European genre, but owned by different companies. The Fountains of Bellagio as seen from the Eiffel Tower are as beautiful as the Eiffel Tower as seen from around the fountains. Working separately, but even better together, the Paris and Bellagio bring class to a place that has long been considered vulgar by many.*

Above: *The Paris cost a whopping $750 million to build, a major portion of that going into the X-shaped, thirty-four-floor Vegasized version of the Hotel de Ville in Paris. But where the Paris city hall overlooks an infamous park once used for executions, the Paris Las Vegas looks out over the circular swimming pool, through the Eiffel Tower, and on to the Fountains of Bellagio. Within those thirty-four floors are 2,916 guest rooms and 295 suites ranging from comfortable to bourgeois. The 85,000-square-foot casino has painted blue skies above, cobblestones underfoot, and the structure of the Eiffel Tower running through it. The Paris Las Vegas has seven restaurants, several bars and lounges, hypnotists, dancers, and a bakery that would make Napoléon say "Ooh la la."*

Left: *The 2001 remake of the 1960 Rat Pack classic* Ocean's Eleven *is a heist picture with the Bellagio Hotel as one of the targets. The movie ends with Danny Ocean's crew staring joyfully into the dancing Fountains of Bellagio, then walking off one by one. The sequel,* Ocean's Twelve, *visits Italy's Lake Como—and there is a connection, as the Bellagio of Las Vegas is modeled on the small Italian resort town of Bellagio, which overlooks Lake Como. This is the effect that Steve Wynn and Mirage Resorts sought when they invested more than $1.6 billion to re-create the middle of the Las Vegas Strip: the oblong, eight-acre man-made lake stands in for the Y-shaped, 36,000-acre Lake Como, and the 3,933 rooms of the Bellagio Hotel could accommodate the 3,000 citizens of Bellagio, Italy, in the marbled luxury to which they are accustomed.*

Above: *Oarsmen, Shooters, Super Shooters, Extreme Shooters. Fancy drinks at the Bank or the Bellagio's Pool Bar? Or something else? The answer is something else, because that is the best description for the musical water show at the Fountains of Bellagio. Built for more than $75 million, the choreographed musical fountains are powered by 1,200 nozzles divided into those four categories—the Super Shooters blast water as high as 460 feet. The fountains are lit by 4,500 lights in the man-made lake. Choreographed to more than a dozen different songs—from Madonna to the Mormon Tabernacle Choir—the Fountains of Bellagio show begins at dusk and goes every thirty minutes until 8:00 and then every fifteen minutes until midnight. The mesmerizing performance of the fountains stops everyone and everything.*

Left: *Looking at the Fountains of Bellagio, one may wonder how all this got here. Water bubbling and springing up out of the ground is at the foundation of Las Vegas. The Paiute Indians knew the area as a constant water source in the middle of a stark and deadly desert. In 1829 the Antonio Armijo expedition was blazing a path from New Mexico to California when eighteen-year-old scout Rafael Rivera went off on his own and found an oasis of water and flora that was marked on the map as "Vegas," or "meadows." When John C. Frémont came through the area in May 1844, he described: "Two narrow streams of clear water, four or five feet deep, gush suddenly with a quick current, from two singularly large springs . . . The taste of the water is good, but rather too warm to be agreeable; the temperature being 71 in the one and 73 in the other. They, however, afford a delightful bathing place." The Mormons built an outpost by Las Vegas Creek in 1855, but the heat and loneliness drove them back to Salt Lake City after three years. Nevada became a state in 1865, and forty years later the abundant water of Las Vegas made it an ideal place to rewater the steam trains of the San Pedro, Los Angeles, and Salt Lake railway. Las Vegas was established as a city in 1911. All of it because of water, and if it seems like Las Vegas celebrates that otherwise common liquid in extravagant ways, just remember—water is at the source of everything.*

Harrah's
IMPERIAL PALACE
CAESARS PALACE

planet

Previous pages: *Mormon icons Donny and Marie Osmond might seem out of place in the middle of Sin City, but the Church of Jesus Christ of Latter-day Saints has a long history in Las Vegas, going back to the first permanent settlement in 1855. By the mid-1960s, Howard Hughes rolled into Las Vegas with his trusted entourage of Mormon executives and assistants. When Hughes was asked to leave his top-floor suites at the Desert Inn, he bought the hotel for $13 million and proceeded to buy half of Las Vegas: Castaways, the Frontier, the Landmark, the Sands, and tens of thousands of acres. Hughes left four years later, after millions of dollars in profits had been skimmed. And then, in 2009, Donny and Marie Osmond followed the Old Mormon Trail to Las Vegas and took over the town with a six-month engagement at the Flamingo.*

Right: *Night is to Las Vegas what makeup is to fashion models: a little bit of magic that diminishes the glare and the flaws, and highlights the glamour. Las Vegas skies are blue and clear, but harsh daylight does not show the best side of the Strip. The hotels and casinos stand high, exposed and vulnerable, uncomfortable in the glare. But then the sun hits a certain point and the glare becomes golden. Las Vegas looks better, feels better, and it seems like the city comes alive as the golden hour fades to black and Las Vegas lights up. This view is taken from behind Planet Hollywood and the Paris Las Vegas, looking west toward CityCenter and the Bellagio, over western Las Vegas to Red Rock Canyon and the last strains of the golden hour.*

Top left: *The Aladdin opened in 1966 with an elaborate sign that was topped by this neon genie's lamp. The sign wasn't as colorful as the Aladdin's history over the next thirty years as it was bought, sold, bankrupted, busted, and opened again—and then imploded in 1998. The new Aladdin opened in 2000, but the troubles continued and the property was bought by Planet Hollywood. The genie's lamp was salvaged from all that, and now stands as part of a walking tour of neon signs on Fremont Street.*

Bottom left: *According to UNLV's Center for Gaming Research Neon Survey, there are many different kinds of neon signs: animated, architectural, backlit, back-to-back, building-front, canopy, cantilever, changeable copy, directional, electronic changeable copy, ground, hanging, internally luminated, LCD, LED, marquee, monument, pole, porte-cochere, projection, pylon, sculpted pylon, super pylon, and upright. Planet Hollywood has almost all of them.*

Right: *Hoteliers have long been importing Hollywood glitz and glamour to the Strip, going back to Billy Wilkerson's vision for the Flamingo Hotel. As seen from across the street at the Bellagio, the fifty floors of Planet Hollywood enclose 2,600 movie-themed rooms and suites, 5,000 plasma TVs, a 7,000-seat theater, a dozen restaurants, and the Miracle Mile Shops, with over 170 retailers. It's all very L.A., right down to Pink's Race and Sports Book Lounge, named for the ever-popular hot dog stand that is a Hollywood legend.*

planet
ph

BALLYS
BALLYS
Jubilee!
Jubilee!
Employee of the Month
Ramon Gonzalez
Runner/Sidewalk Café
Congratulations on a Job Well Done!
BALLY'S
Employee of the Month
Ramon Gonzalez
Runner/Sidewalk Café
Congratulations on a Job Well Done!
BALLY'S
ked to depression
NBA LIVE UPDATE
BALLYS
A TRIBUTE TO QUEEN
160
PENN

Left: *The pedestrian bridge from the Bellagio over Las Vegas Boulevard connects to a short escalator leading down to the People Mover, which transports citizens just about 400 feet from the sidewalk to the many wonders that await within Bally's Hotel and Casino.*

Above: *The People Mover also connects to the Bally's/Paris Las Vegas station of the Las Vegas Monorail. Opened in 2004, the monorail carries an average of 20,000 passengers a day for 3.6 miles from the MGM Grand in the south to Bally's/Paris, Flamingo/Caesars Palace, Harrah's/ Imperial Palace, the convention center, the Las Vegas Hilton, and the northern terminus at the Sahara station. There are plans to extend the monorail to McCarran International Airport, but one can only imagine what Las Vegas's rental car, taxi, and limo industries think about that.*

CAESARS PALACE
CAESARS PALACE

Left: *Caesars Palace opened in 1966, the marbleized reality of Jay Sarno, who wanted to bring European class to the Strip. On December 31, 1967, Evel Knievel put Caesars Palace into legend and himself in traction when he attempted to jump his Triumph Bonneville 151 feet over this fountain. His motorcycle lost power just before takeoff, which meant Knievel landed short, lost control, hit the pavement, and rolled over and over in one of the worst accidents ever caught on film (by Linda Evans, as a matter of fact). Knievel broke bones from toes to head, and suffered a concussion that put him in a coma for almost a month. The daredevil lived to crash another day, and Caesars Palace began with a saga as wildly spectacular as anything Rome ever produced.*

Above right: *What chariot racing was to Rome, NASCAR is to Las Vegas: the power of two wild horses as opposed to 500-horsepower engines—but just as exciting. This is Caesar himself, spurring his steeds on to victory. The crowds at the Las Vegas Motor Speedway go just as nuts as the Romans did in the Colosseum.*

Below right: *Neptune is the Roman god of water and the sea, but this isn't him. This is one of two retainers at the feet of the outdoor statue of the water god, overlooking the Neptune Fountain. This member of Neptune's posse is charged with playing soothing music on the conch, while the other keeps Neptune's sea horses steady.*

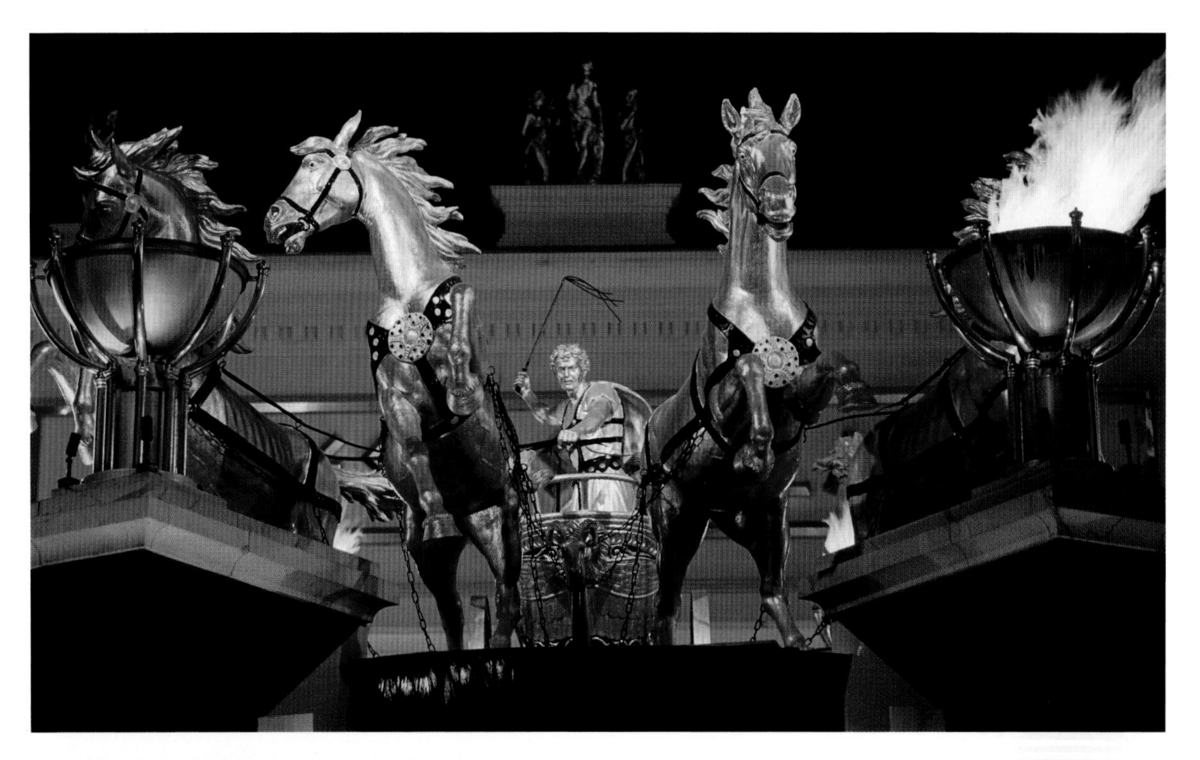

Left: *Dressed in the robes of the imperator—commander of the Roman army—Augustus Caesar addresses a crowd, perhaps about the severe shortage of child care in Rome. The original statue of Augustus Caesar—adopted by his uncle Julius Caesar—was found in 1863 and is now at the Vatican. The replica at Caesars Palace is to scale, and stands at the entrance driveway welcoming one and all to Caesars Palace—infants included. (Actually, the infant is Cupid, the son of Venus, a symbol of divine lineage from the goddess of love and beauty.)*

Right: *The size, scale, luxury, and grandeur of Caesars Palace was always meant to elicit the awe that Romans felt when they walked through the streets of Rome and to the Colosseum: "I did not know men could build such things." The original Caesars Palace, opened in 1966, had 680 rooms in the fourteen-floor Roman Tower. And then, like Rome, it grew. The fourteen-story, 222-room Centurion Tower and Cleopatra's Barge were added in 1970. The Roman Tower was extended in 1973. The twenty-two-story Forum Tower opened in 1979. The Forum Shops opened in 1992. The Palace Tower and Second Wing Forum Shops were added in 1997. In 2000 the facades of all the older buildings were upgraded to reflect the style of the newer towers and mall. The Colosseum Theater opened in 2003. The Augustus Tower added a meeting facility in 2004. The Octavius Tower's three luxury pool villa suites opened in 2009. Caesars Palace now has 3,350 rooms, including luxury suites like the Royal Suite, two-story Emperor Suites, Senator Suites, Palace Tower King Suites, and penthouses spanning 10,000 to 12,500 square feet. The Absolut Suite spans 1,800 square feet of luxury inspired by six flavors of Absolut Vodka—perfect for your next bacchanal.*

CAESARS PALACE
CAESARS PALACE

BILL'S
GAMBLIN' HALL
& SALOON
Drai's
BALLYS

Left: *Bill's Gamblin' Hall and Saloon was named for Bill Harrah, who began in the gaming business in the 1920s with a variation on bingo called the Circle Game. A California native, he was driven out by all those pesky laws, and opened Harrah's Club Bingo in Reno in 1937. That was the start of what became the largest gaming company in the world, with yearly revenues exceeding $10 billion. In 2007 Harrah's traded properties with Boyd Gaming and ended up with the Barbary Coast Hotel and Casino, which had stood on that corner of East Flamingo Road and Las Vegas Boulevard since 1979. Looking to rebrand it, Harrah's named it in honor of its founder.*

Above: *What Bill's Gamblin' Hall and Saloon lacks in size, it makes up for in its location at one of the hottest corners on the Strip: East Flamingo and Las Vegas Boulevard, between the Flamingo and Bally's, across the bridge from Caesars Palace. The plan is to expand the Flamingo into that building, but for now Bill's is going strong: a small, 197-room hotel with personal service and good food. You can go to Bill's Lounge to check out an Elvis Presley impersonator, or relax in the chic after-hours nightclub at Drai's. Low table minimums attract many to the 20,000-square-foot casino that is one-tenth the size of the casino at the Venetian, which, at 225,000 square feet, is the largest casino on the Strip.*

Flamingo
Flamingo

Left: *The Flamingo Hotel is forever linked with the name of Benjamin "Bugsy" Siegel, but the truth is, the 1940s hotel/casino was originally dreamed up by Billy Wilkerson, who founded the Hollywood Reporter and other famous nightclubs. Siegel got involved when Wilkerson ran out of money. As a trusted executive/executor/executionist of Lucky Luciano and Meyer Lansky, Siegel moved up from teenage thug to New York hit man to a West Coast agent for the East Coast syndicate: taking pieces of the race-wire business, establishing drug-running ties with Mexico, with his hands in prostitution and gambling. And that included Las Vegas: "In a sense he was the Christopher Columbus for the mob," Wallace Turner wrote in his 1965 book* Gamblers' Money. *"He went exploring and found the New World in the desert." Siegel invested $1.5 million Mafia dollars into the Flamingo and became a controlling partner. Wilkerson had Hollywood ideas for the Flamingo, while Siegel saw it as a Miami-inspired "carpet joint." Siegel demanded many modifications and renovations to the Flamingo, which meant it opened rough and unfinished on December 26, 1946. In June 1947, Siegel was assassinated by a never-identified hit man armed with an army carbine. Siegel's ideas for the Flamingo as a class joint resonate to this day, but the gruesome photos and headlines from his murder did as much for Las Vegas's image as Sin City as the Flamingo did for all the hotels and casinos to come.*

Following pages: *The middle of the Strip, from the northeast, looking toward the southwest over the back of the Flamingo, along Bally's and toward the Paris Las Vegas, the Bellagio, and CityCenter. If only Siegel could see Las Vegas now.*

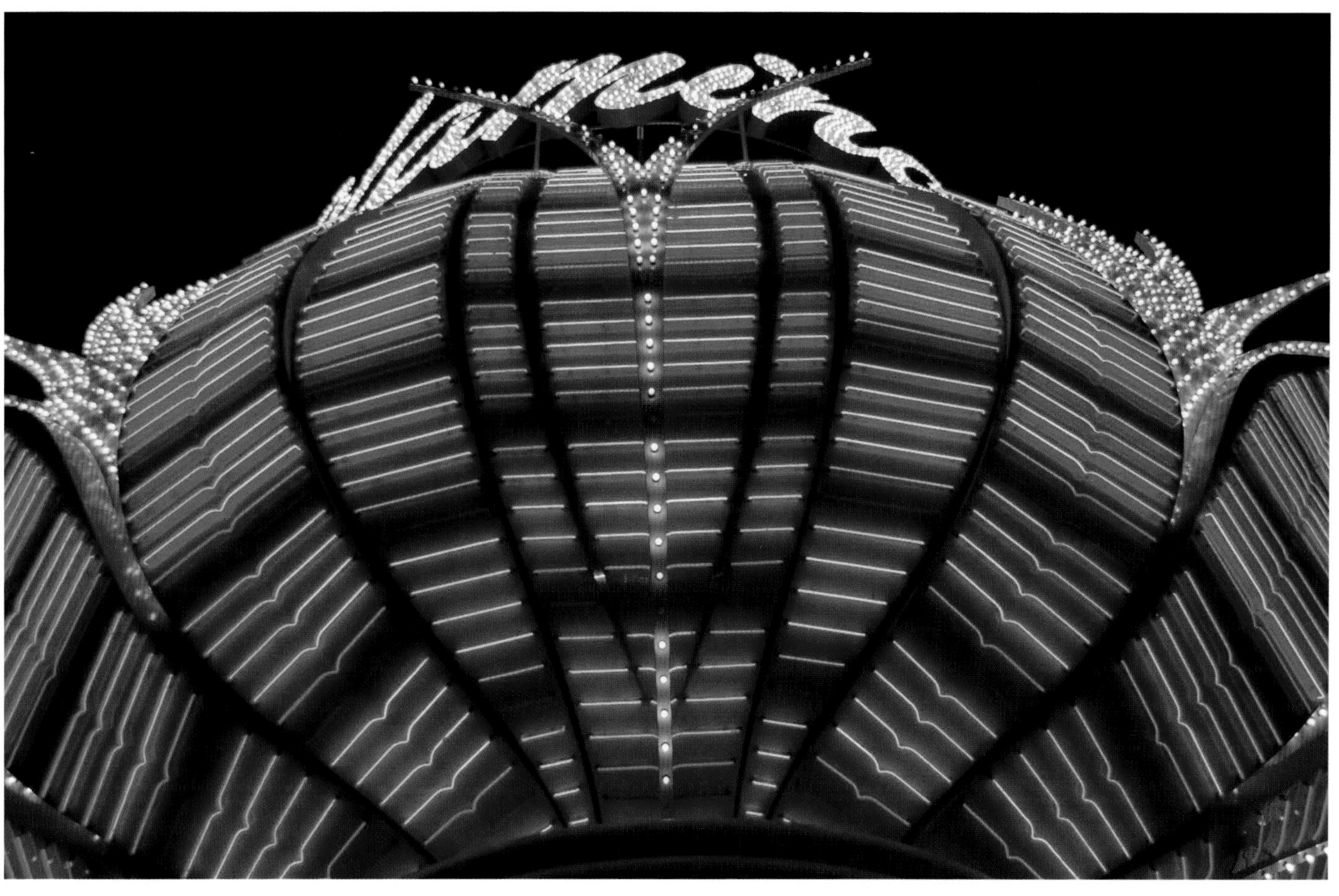

Flamingo

Right: *Las Vegas history divides into "Before the Mirage" and "After the Mirage," with the dividing line at November 22, 1989, when Steve Wynn opened his $630 million investment: "More than a business opportunity or a chance to make more bucks," Wynn was quoted as saying. "This is a vote of confidence for Nevada and Las Vegas." The Mirage ended a slow era for Las Vegas that went back to 1976, when gambling was made legal in Atlantic City, New Jersey, diverting a tremendous amount of business to the East Coast and shaking confidence in Las Vegas as a destination or an investment. Howard Hughes died in 1976, Elvis Presley died a year later, and in 1980 a fire at the MGM Grand killed eighty-seven people. The failed car bombing of Frank "Lefty" Rosenthal in 1982 and the murder of Anthony "the Ant" Spilotro in 1986 made national headlines and kept the mobster aura around Sin City (and inspired the Martin Scorsese movie* Casino*). From the 1970s and into the 1980s, Las Vegas had a confidence problem and needed a hero. Working with Michael Milken, who raised $600 million in financing, Wynn directed the construction of a "megaresort" with 1.1 million square feet of public area and 3,044 rooms. The Mirage was designed as a South Seas tropical fantasy: water everywhere, pools, waterfalls, white tigers, dolphins, a lot of jungle greenery, and even a volcano out front, which exploded every fifteen minutes. The first guests allowed into the Mirage were four white tigers, and they were followed soon after by Siegfried and Roy, an act that was one of the biggest draws on the Strip from 1990 to 2003. The Mirage was the first major casino built in sixteen years. Its success revitalized Las Vegas and inspired the many casinos that sprung up in the 1990s.*

THE MIRAGE
THE BEATLES
LOVE
BY CIRQUE DU SOLEIL

Left: *The Mirage volcano originally went off every seven minutes, but the show caused so much gawker traffic on the Strip, the hotel's management adjusted the schedule to every fifteen minutes. With the volcano, the gold windows, and Siegfried and Roy, the Mirage stood out as the next big thing on the Strip, but by the end of the 1990s it had been hemmed in by all the megaresorts that followed. In December 2008, the Mirage unveiled a new volcano show: fireballs burst twelve feet into the air, spouts of water go even higher, and it's all flame and color erupting and dancing to the drumming of the Grateful Dead's Mickey Hart and Indian tabla master Zakir Hussain. The music is true to the South Pacific theme, and the light and heat of the show are mesmerizing. The Mirage volcano now erupts every hour on the hour.*

THE MIRAGE
THE MIRAGE
THE MIRAGE
Coca-Cola

Left: *The Mirage Hotel and Casino is accessible from the Strip under two golden arches that reflect the South Pacific theme—rainbows are an everyday occurrence in the tropics, although golden rainbows are rare.*

Above: *The golden hour is that period when the sun is setting at just the right angle to turn all that harsh daylight into regal shades of purple and gold. It is a time of day when all of Las Vegas lets out a collective "Ahh!" because the workday is over and it's time to hit the casinos. That hour is golden to the casinos, but some, like the Mirage, keep the golden hour going all night long. The gold tint on the facade of the Mirage is no trick: the windows are tinted with actual gold.*

Harrahs

Left: *The seven-starred globe on top of Harrah's Las Vegas is the old company logo. The present inventory of Harrah's holdings is now an entire constellation. What began as a small bingo hall in Reno has become one of the largest gaming companies in the world. On the Las Vegas Strip, Harrah's has built or bought Harrah's Las Vegas, Caesars Palace, the Paris Las Vegas, the Rio All Suite Hotel and Casino, the Flamingo Las Vegas, Bally's Las Vegas, and the Imperial Palace. Harrah's bought Binion's Horseshoe in 2004 and then sold it in 2005, but retained rights to the World Series of Poker.*

Top right: *What opened as the Holiday Casino in 1973 was renamed Harrah's in 1992 and remodeled in 1997. Out went the showboat theme and in came a complete remodel around the carnival theme. Harrah's has 2,587 hotel rooms and ninety hotel suites in three towers: the Mardi Gras North Tower, the Mardi Gras South Tower, and the Carnaval Tower.*

Below right: *The Asian influence can be seen and not seen all around Las Vegas. The lion that once stood at the entrance to the MGM Grand is no longer there, due to Chinese beliefs. The same is true for no floors numbered starting with 4 at the Wynn and Encore because, in Chinese, the word for "four" rhymes with the word for "death." Asian games can be found all around Las Vegas, and it would not be surprising if one of the megaresorts of the future took on an Asian theme. But gambling is not new to Asia, and the Imperial Palace is not a new resort cashing in on the flow of gamblers from the Orient. The Imperial Palace was built over the bones of the Flamingo Capri and opened in 1979. They added an eighteen-story tower in 1988, and Harrah's bought the property in 2005. Plans to raze the building were set aside, and Harrah's has invested millions to make the hotel and casino even more palatial.*

Following pages: *Bright lights, big city, setting souls on fire. Northeast of the Strip, looking southwest over the back of the Imperial Palace toward Caesars Palace, the Rio Las Vegas, and the Palms Casino Resort.*

PALMS
PALMS
CAESARS PALACE
TELLER
IMPERIAL PALACE

Rio
Rio
Harrah's
PHANTOM
SUSHI

Above and right: *If signage and branding are attitude in Las Vegas, then the Casino Royale is a boutique casino with attitude. In a prime spot between Harrah's and the Venetian and across from the Mirage, the Casino Royale is a vintage 1990s casino that uses the old-school technique of street barkers to lure patrons. As a further incentive, there's the promise of 100-1 odds at craps. Is it working? The Casino Royale opened in 1992 and it's still there, over the bones of the Nob Hill Casino, which lasted only a year, from 1989 to 1990.*

CASINO
ROYALE

Left: *Treasure Island opened in 1993 with a pirate theme intended to provide fun for the whole family. Treasure Island is where the Cirque du Soleil first performed and inspired a whole new level of Las Vegas shows. In 2003 Treasure Island rebranded itself as "ti," moving away from the whole family and toward adults. It now features bars and hot tubs instead of arcades and kiddie pools.*

Below: *The pirate theme is a perfect metaphor for Las Vegas business. The town was founded by rascals and rogues, and the corporate privateers who run the town now are constantly invading each other's property, flying new colors, scuttling plans and developments, imploding buildings, and replacing them with bigger ones. Steve Wynn built Treasure Island for $450 million in 1993, and it was sold to MGM in 2000. And then, from over the horizon, came the buccaneer Phil Ruffin. In 1999 Ruffin bought the Frontier Hotel and Casino—formerly Guy McAfee's 91 Club—and changed the name to the New Frontier. Ruffin ran the New Frontier until it was scuttled in November 2007. He sold the thirty-six-acre patch of dirt for $1.2 billion and was part of a partnership with Donald Trump in Trump Tower. Flush with cash, Ruffin bought Treasure Island in 2008 for $775 million.*

Right: *The pirate show at Buccaneer Bay was intended to be a kid-friendly attraction when it opened in 1999. Buccaneer Bay was a family-friendly show—a classic face-off of privateers and sailors: cannons blasting, men jumping overboard or swinging from ropes with swords in their teeth to do dastardly or heroic deeds. The bad guys sink, the good guys win. Buccaneer Bay might have been violent and loud and hot, but it was fun for the whole family. Buccaneer Bay was always a hot show, as the exploding cannonballs put out impressive gouts of flame and a heat you could feel on your face. But the show got even hotter when Treasure Island transformed itself into "ti." What was Buccaneer Bay became Sirens of ti. The new show features a crew of bustier-clad buccaneer bad girls who lure renegade booty-seeking cutthroat pirates into Siren's Cove, mesmerize them with their singing and dancing, and then finish them off with cannon fire. The girls win, the boys sink. Sirens of ti gives passersby a taste of what a big Vegas show is like and whets their appetite.*

Below right: *In the Sirens of ti show, cannons fire, flames burst, and men who can't take the heat jump overboard. The sirens sing and dance. This show is free, and goes off four times a night, every night along the Strip. The heat from this is even more intense than that of the Mirage volcano.*

VENETIAN
THE VENETIAN
RESORT · HOTEL · CASINO

Left: *The Sands Hotel is where the Rat Pack ruled in 1960, and it was considered one of the coolest hotel/casinos on the Strip—the Queen of Las Vegas—in its long life from 1952 to its implosion in 1996. Where the Queen of Las Vegas once stood, the Queen of the Adriatic resides now. Three years and a $1 billion investment later, on May 3, 1999, Italian icon Sophia Loren was on hand to open Las Vegas's new Italian icon: the Venetian Las Vegas. Modeled after Venice, Italy—the Queen of the Adriatic—the Venetian has 3,014 suites ranging in size from 650 to 8,000 square feet. The 120,000-square-foot casino has one of the largest poker rooms on the Strip, and when all of that is combined with the Palazzo Hotel and Casino Resort and the Sands Expo Convention Center, the Venetian adds its rooms and space to the world's largest hotel and resort complex.*

Right: *Similar to New York–New York, the Venetian clusters many of the famous architectural landmarks of the 159-square-mile Venice archipelago into a smaller area: the Rialto Bridge, Saint Mark's Campanile, the Bridge of Sighs, fountains, statues, and oodles of marble. Just as Saint Mark's Square is framed by art galleries, the Venetian is home to Madame Tussauds and has hosted exhibits from the Guggenheim. The Rialto Bridge in Venice is lined with shops selling jewelry, art, embroidery, and other fine things that Venetians crave. The same is true for the Venetian, which is a shopper's paradise. Authentic Venetian gondolas wind along the Grand Canal, past shops and gawkers, into the hotel and out again. This all could have been pretentious, gauche, vulgar, or whatever you want to call it. But this is the new Vegas, which does things right, with class.*

Right: *The people of Venice are as protective of their city as Las Vegans. When Lucia Daniella Griggi, a native of Venice, visited the Venetian in 2009, she expected to be insulted. And yet: "I was blown away," Lucia said after. "By the authenticity, by the sheer size and the attention to detail. The only thing missing were the pigeons—which is good—and the ocean breeze and the constant Vivaldi—and how the heat falls on your back when you turn into the art galleries." As protective as Venetians might be, there is little they can do to protect their beautiful city from the creeping threat of global warming—which could inundate the Queen of the Adriatic and leave it to the ghosts and the pigeons. According to PBS's* Nova, *where Saint Mark's Square was impassable due to high tides except for only a handful of times at the turn of the nineteenth century into the twentieth, by 1986 there were forty instances of* acqua alta, *or "high water," turning Saint Mark's Square into a shallow lake. By 1996 the guards had to sandbag the Doge's Palace ninety-nine times. Those numbers make Venetians nervous about the fate of their city. If the sum of all fears results in Venice being made impassable due to a permanent acqua alta, many facets of Venice are preserved in Las Vegas, which won't be threatened by high tides anytime soon.*

Right: *In Venice, the Palazzo Ducale di Venezia overlooks Saint Mark's Square—the residence of the doge: a magistrate elected for life by the Venetian aristocracy. The Doge's Palace was built on the cusp of the fourteenth and fifteenth centuries and has survived as a classic of Gothic architecture. Criminals entering the Doge's Palace through the front entrance sometimes never again saw the light of day, as they were led over the Bridge of Sighs to the dungeons of Venice. Venetian legend says that lovers who kiss under the Bridge of Sighs at sunset will have eternal love. At the Venetian, a bridge over the Grand Canal leads from the Strip to a replica of the Doge's Palace and transports visitors out of the rattle and hum of the twenty-first century and back to the romance of medieval Venice.*

Right: *Saint Mark's Campanile is the bell tower for Saint Mark's Basilica—an ornate, domed Byzantine structure that served as the main cathedral of Venice going back to the ninth century. The original tower dates to 1514, but it was rebuilt in 1912 after it self-imploded due to cracks that appeared in 1902. The original is 323 feet high and overlooks Saint Mark's Square in Venice. The reproduction in Las Vegas is to scale and overlooks a bit of the Grand Canal and the bridge to the Doge's Palace. Saint Mark's Campanile in Venice is a bell tower, and the five bells each represented a different event: a bell for executions, a bell to announce sessions of the senate, a bell to mark midday, a bell to call the members of the Maggior Consiglio to council meetings, and the loudest bell to mark the beginning and end of the working day. Las Vegas doesn't want people within the casinos to know what time of day it is outside, so the bell tower at the Venetian does not mark time. But the campanile marks the location of the Venetian, as it is a landmark that stands out amid all the height and visual clutter of the Strip. The Campanile di San Marco does not allow tours up into the bell tower, and the same goes for Las Vegas. The reproduction of the famous Venice landmark has to be worshipped from below—or above—but never from within.*

SPIRITUAL
DINING
TAO
NIGHTCLUB
RELIGIOUS
NIGHTLIFE

Right: *Sister to the Venetian and one-third of the Sands Megacenter, the Palazzo had a "soft opening" on December 30, 2007, and then a grand opening on January 17, 2008. The Palazzo under construction is where Al Pacino and Elliot Gould were filmed in* Ocean's Thirteen*. The construction of the Palazzo was a miracle of modern engineering. The Palazzo squeezed 7.5 million square feet of rooms, suites, casino, shops, and restaurants into an eight-acre site. That process began by removing 1.2 million cubic yards of dirt to build a sixty-foot-deep, 4,000-space subterranean parking garage: as many as 600 trucks a day, six days a week, for a total of 114,285 truck trips. On top of that, a steel-framed, environmentally state-of-the-art building rose at the rate of one floor a week—and $2 million a day—to top out at fifty floors. There are 3,042 rooms in the Palazzo, which is not themed like the Venetian or other hotels but styled after Rodeo Drive, Beverly Hills, and Bel Air. It has a 105,000-square-foot casino, a 2,000-seat theater, a 450,000-square-foot convention center, and a 72,000-square-foot grand ballroom that can accommodate 2,500 people. The shopping mall has 450,000 square feet for high-end retail, from Barneys New York to Lamborghini. They used 1.8 million square feet of stone, including 11,000 tons of Irish green stone and Egyptian marble. Forty-five pools and water features are included, as well as forty-five chandeliers, a fifty-foot-high marble chalice that flows 50,000 gallons of water, and a 3,000-pound chandelier over the Gold Bar, which is fifteen feet in diameter. All of that in forty-one months, for $1.8 billion. The creation of the Palazzo was a miracle of modern engineering, construction finesse, and speed.*

TRUMP
TREASURE ISLAND
MIRAGE
RAGE

Left: *Hovering at almost column level over Caesars Palace, looking north along the Strip, the business of Las Vegas breaks down like this: The deal that made the Trump Hotel helped Phil Ruffin buy Treasure Island. Steve Wynn made his bones with the Mirage, which led to his development of the Encore and Wynn. And it was Wynn's success with the Bellagio that led to the European-themed Venetian and Palazzo.*

Following pages: *Hovering over Treasure Island looking south along the Strip. In February 2001, Steve Wynn summed up views like this: "What I love the most about this town is the terrific opportunity it presents to those with the imagination and daring to build new must-see properties. Where else could you find a pyramid next to Camelot, next to the Statue of Liberty and Monte Carlo, an Italian lake next to the Roman Empire? Here this madness is okay. Anyplace else, they'd lock you up. The best is yet to come. The next five years will see a renaissance of entertainment here."*

MIRAGE
BEATLES
LOVE
CAESARS PALACE
MIRAGE
CASINO & RESORT
LOVE
TERRY FATOR
Harrah's
Rita Rudner

FASHIONSHOW
FASHIONSHOW

Left: *What looks like an impaled flying saucer is actually "the Cloud"—an elliptical steel superstructure 460 feet long suspended twenty stories above the entrance to the Fashion Show Mall. The Fashion Show is a retail and restaurant center that opened in 1981. Covering nearly two million square feet, the Fashion Show is a Vegasized indoor mall anchored by eight department stores, 250 retail shops, a dozen restaurants, and an eighty-foot-long runway and stage that floats up out of the mall floor, where regular weekend fashion shows take place. The Cloud provides shade in the daytime, and at night it is a projection screen for ads, events, light shows, and dreams.*

Right: *Le Rêve was the original name for this hotel: the culmination of all of Steve Wynn's dreams coming true. Wynn took over the family bingo parlor in Maryland and made enough money to move to Las Vegas with his wife, Elaine, and buy a piece of the Frontier Hotel and Casino. Wynn ran a liquor and wine importing company from 1968 to 1972, and then made enough in a land deal involving Howard Hughes and Caesars Palace to buy the controlling interest in the Golden Nugget on Fremont Street. Another seventeen years in Las Vegas and Wynn had the confidence to back the Mirage, a $600 million megaresort that revitalized the Strip and launched the building boom of the 1990s. Wynn then opened the Treasure Island Hotel and Casino in 1993. His next project was the Bellagio—which again inspired a new genre of massive luxury hotels on the Strip: the Venetian, Mandalay Bay, and the Paris Las Vegas. In 2000 Mirage Resorts was sold to MGM for $6.6 billion, giving Wynn $600 million in personal financial clout to build his dream hotel, Le Rêve. Despite the $2.7 billion cost, "he hid the waterfalls, puppets and giant screens behind man-made mountains," Joel Stein wrote for* Time *magazine in 2006. Wynn went for classic black, with the accent on class. But as Le Rêve was coming true, Wynn decided that a word that sounded like "win" would be a more inspiring name.*

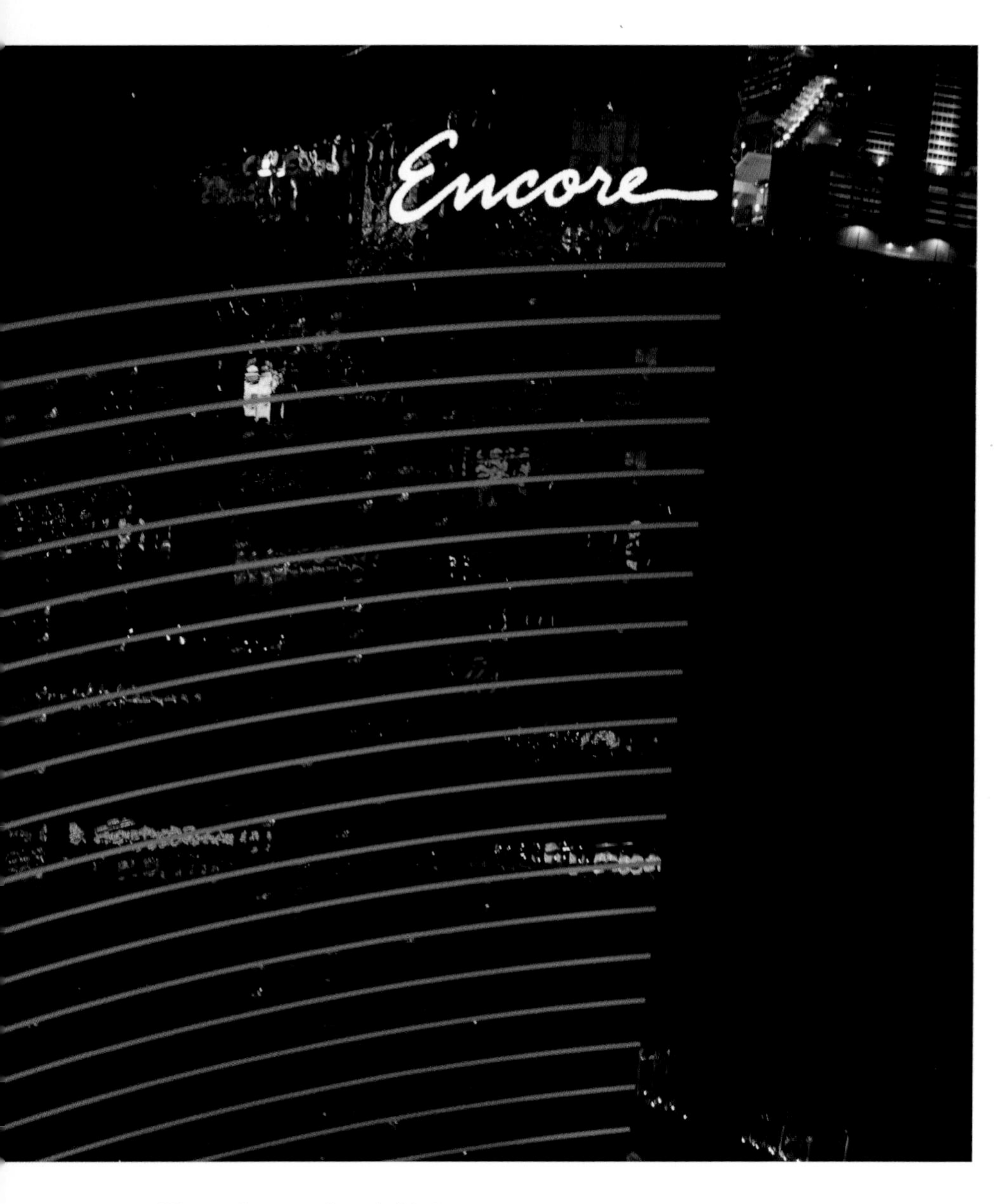

Above: *"Encore" means "again" in French, and that is how Steve Wynn celebrated the success of the Wynn Hotel—by building its twin sister, the Encore Suites. The Encore cost another $2 billion and it opened its 2,074 suites—to the tune of Sinatra's "Luck Be a Lady Tonight"—on December 22, 2008, just in time for the massive economic downturn. The Encore's management reduced room prices but not services and decided to ride it out.*

Right: *The Wynn and the Encore Suites share facilities—including a lavish golf course in the back—and they are connected by a retail channel. The Encore is three stories taller than the Wynn, and while the two hotels have their differences, as all sisters do, they share one quirk: neither hotel has floors that start with the number 4, because that number, in Chinese, rhymes with the word for "death."*

Left: *In feng shui, flowing water represents wealth, and Las Vegas celebrates/flaunts/displays/distributes its water wealth in many ways: fountains, water traps, wave pools, aquariums, canals, waterfalls, streams, marbeled bathtubs, hot tubs, and spas. Some are for form, some are for function, but form and function come together beautifully in the pools along the Strip, from private suites hidden away on rooftops to the public pools that are oh-so-popular on a blazing summer day. This is the guest pool at the Wynn Resort, between the main building and the golf course. Surrounded by deck chairs and cabanas, it's the perfect place to cool off on a hot day, in those long, restless hours between sleeping and gaming.*

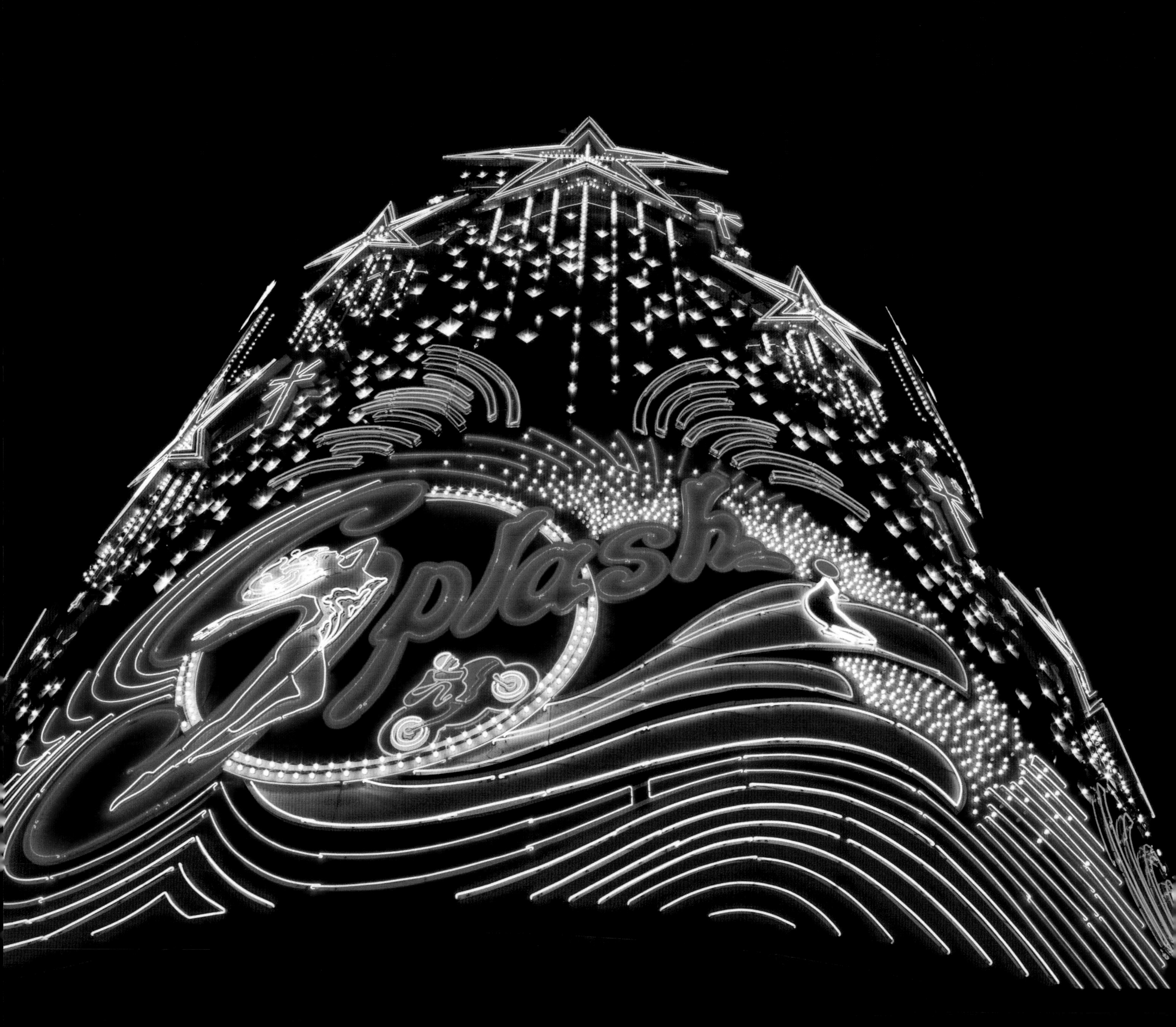
Splash

Left: *When the Riviera opened in 1955, it was the ninth hotel/casino built on the Strip—and the first high-rise. Like any casino that has been around that long, the Riviera has a lot of famous names attached to it, from Joan Crawford and Liberace (who was the hotel's opening act) to Harpo and Zeppo Marx and Dean Martin (who were partial owners) to the Rat Pack in the 1960s and all the way to Michael Myers, who starred in* Austin Powers: International Man of Mystery, *which was shot at the Riviera. Once a casino turns fifty, it starts to experience thoughts and emotions similar to humans: How do I look? Where are my friends? Will I be replaced? Many of the casinos and hotels the Riviera grew up with are gone: the Landmark, the Aladdin, the Thunderbird. The huge vacant dirt lot across the Strip used to be the Stardust and the Westward Ho, but they were imploded to make way for the Echelon, which has a price tag of $4 billion.*

Top right: *A hotel/casino in Las Vegas collects a lot of signs in fifty-plus years, and the Riviera doesn't seem to want to let any of them go. This two-story electric structure is at the southeast corner of the hotel, and serves to advertise both the place and the shows going on within.*

Bottom right: *The Riviera has had a lot of legendary Las Vegas performers and shows over the years: Liberace, Splash, and An Evening at La Cage, featuring female impersonator Frank Marino. This statue outside the hotel is a tribute to Crazy Girls: "Las Vegas's Sexiest Topless Revue."*

Left and right: *Rio de Janeiro does things differently. There is no other city like it in the world—a big, uninhibited, libertine European-style city between the jungle and the deep blue sea. Picking up on that, the Rio All Suite Hotel and Casino is a Brazilian-themed hotel/casino that dared to be different when it opened in 1992. Almost a mile off the Strip, it features glass elevators on the outside, a red-and-purple color scheme, and was the first hotel in Las Vegas to offer all suites. Since its opening, the Rio has scored a couple of coups. It hosted the World Series of Poker in 2005, although the final three tables went back to Binion's. In 2006 the Rio booked Prince to play regular shows every Friday and Saturday night at the 3121 Club. Prince began in November 2006 and continued until March 2007, and his reign at the Rio was seen by many as eliminating once and for all the aura of Vegas as a place where tired acts went to die.*

CIRCUS CIRCUS
CIRCUS CIRCUS
FREE CIRCUS ACTS
SLOTS A FUN
McDonald's

Left: *Circus Circus was opened by Jay Sarno in 1968, and it was going strong when Hunter Thompson came to town in 1971. The gonzo writer was less than flattering in his book* Fear and Loathing in Las Vegas*: "The Circus Circus is what the whole hep world would be doing Saturday night if the Nazis had won the war." The original Circus Circus was under a tent-shaped building that remains the largest permanent big top in the world. Trapeze artists performed overhead while a pink elephant went around and around on a tram. Hunter Thompson saw things he didn't like, but Jay Sarno's vision launched Circus Circus Enterprises, which went on to own or build some of Las Vegas's most audacious hotel/casinos.*

Above: *Like a circus performer, Circus Circus went up and out. The Casino Tower was built in 1973 and expanded in 1975, when the porte cochere (which means "coach door" in French) was connected to the big top and the 126-foot Lucky the Clown sign went up. The Circusland RV Park was added in 1979, and is still going. In 1981 a 1,500-foot monorail connected the main hotel to Circus Circus Manor. This area behind the main tower was called Grand Slam Canyon when it opened in 1993, but is now the Adventuredome: "Five Acres of Indoor Fun," where kids can go for a spin on the Disk'O, the Canyon Blaster, the Rim Runner, the Sling Shot, and the ever-popular SpongeBob SquarePants 4-D ride in the SimEx Theater.*

Left: *As much an icon of Las Vegas glamour as Sinatra and Elvis, beautiful women wearing exotic headwear goes back to the 1950s, when the Folies Bergere, Lido de Paris, the Copa Girls, the Latin Quarter Revue, Casino de Paris, and dozens of other shows sprang up around town. Some of these shows were imported from France, others were created out of the dust of the desert. Minsky's Follies upped the ante by going topless, and since then it's been an in-your-face race for bigger and more extravagant shows. Originally, Las Vegas entertainment was a feathered lure to bait gamblers into hotels and casinos. Now, entertainment stands on its own. Typical of the new wave of shows hitting the Strip is "LOVE," the Cirque du Soleil's interpretation of the Beatles' music at the Mirage. Pictured left, an aerialist from the spectacular long-running production.*

Right: *The desert theme isn't too much of a stretch in the Las Vegas Valley, and the Sahara's "nights in Morocco" styling is in the same genre as the Desert Inn, the Dunes, and the Sands. Built in 1952, the Sahara is a Las Vegas legend in so many ways: Louis Prima was the lounge act at the Sahara, Abbott and Costello ended their partnership there, Ocean's Eleven was filmed on the grounds, the Beatles and Bill Cosby performed there, and Jerry Lewis held his Labor Day telethons at the Sahara in the 1970s and 1980s. Many hotel/casinos of Sahara vintage have been imploded and returned to the dust of the desert. The Sahara has stayed current by hitching its wagon to NASCAR. One of the biggest thrills on the Strip is Speed: The Ride, a NASCAR-themed roller coaster that goes as fast as seventy miles per hour, in and out of the Sahara and back again.*

SAHARA

Right: *Architects have had a lot of fun with Las Vegas over the years, and one of the things they have had fun with is buildings like this, which combine the function of protecting new arrivals and departures with whatever form fits the building it's attached to. The porte cochere protects guests from the elements, and while Las Vegas is generally a benign desert environment, during the summer the heat is extreme, and winters can get cold. February is the wettest month with a dam-busting average of 0.69 inch, while the average high temperature in June and July is well over a hundred degrees. And despite all the pools, fountains, lagoons, and other water holes brought in, that is a dry heat. Las Vegas has rain and heat, but also wind and dust and sometimes even hail and snow. The porte cochere located at the entrances aren't entirely there for style, although this structure at the Sahara makes an exotic first impression for anyone pulling in.*

Left and above: *At ground level, citizens use the Stratosphere Tower as an aid to navigation. No matter where you go, there it is, and just by finding the Stratosphere you know where in Las Vegas you are. The original plan for a superlative, Vegasized tower—1,800 feet high to make it the world's tallest structure at the time—was scaled down in the early 1990s by FAA authorities and officials at McCarran International Airport, who saw it as a potential hazard to air traffic. The Stratosphere Tower is only half as tall as the world's tallest structure today, the Burj Dubai at 2,684 feet, but at 1,149 feet, the Stratosphere is by far the tallest structure in Las Vegas. The Stratosphere is the second tower hotel in Las Vegas, following the Landmark Hotel, which struggled to scrape the sky from 1969 to 1995, but was imploded and toppled. While under construction in 1993, a fire threatened to send a crane toppling to the valley floor. The Stratosphere Tower opened in April 1996, built over Bob Stupak's Vegas World, which opened in 1979. The Stratosphere is on Las Vegas Boulevard but on the north side of Sahara Avenue, which means it's not technically on the Strip. Because the Stratosphere is within the city limits of Las Vegas, the Nevada Gaming Commission groups it with the downtown casinos. This view is from the southwest, looking north by northeast toward Fremont Street and Nellis Air Force Base.*

Above: *Dinner, views, and thrills at the top. At the base, the Stratosphere hotel/ casino. There are 2,044 reasonably priced rooms and a casino that makes up its own rules: crapless craps as well as double-exposure blackjack, where you see both the dealer's cards but pushes pay the dealer. And if you're into dancing vampires, the Stratosphere's racy revue will be your perfect night out.*

Right: *Ear- and eye-popping, the Stratosphere Tower is 113 stories, although most of the action is at the top. The restaurant is called Top of the World, and it revolves 360 degrees to give a spectacular view of Las Vegas, from the Strip to the south, the sun setting over Mount Charleston in the west, downtown and Fremont Street to the north, and Nellis Air Force Base to the northeast. And if you have ever wanted to see fireworks exploding at eye level, the Stratosphere Tower is the place to be on the Fourth of July.*

CIRCUS
CIRCUS

Previous pages: *Visitors can ride up the Stratosphere and hop onto three thrill rides at the top. One, Insanity, dangles riders sixty-four feet out from the edge of the platform and twirls them around, 900 feet above the ground. In 2002 the owners of the Stratosphere proposed a roller coaster that would drop several hundred feet from the tower to street level. Neighbors protested, however, so the plan never materialized.*

Right: *Fremont Street was the original red-light district for Las Vegas, but by the 1940s, the Strip began a high-stakes competition with Fremont Street to determine which was Las Vegas's main drag. By the 1990s, the Strip had claimed that title, and Fremont Street was in need of a makeover. In June 1992, architect Jon Jerde proposed a plan to turn Fremont Street into a pedestrian walkway and cover it all with a lighted, musical dome. Three years and more than $70 million later, the Fremont Street Experience opened in December 1995.*

Left: *"The Hacienda Horse and Rider" welcomed one and all to the Hacienda Hotel, which opened in 1955. The Hacienda was imploded in 1996 to make way for Mandalay Bay, but the sign was saved and preserved and now stands at the juncture of Las Vegas Boulevard and the Fremont Street Experience. The lighting of the Hacienda Horse and Rider celebrated the opening of the Neon Museum in November 1996.*

Right: *Where Fremont Street was once covered in a blanket of stars that was drowned out by all the neon lights, it is now covered in a canopy ninety feet high and more than 1,400 feet long, which uses 12.5 million LED bulbs to put on a dazzling, pedestrian-stopping light-and-sound extravaganza. The Viva Vision canopy is effectively the world's largest and most expensive television set, having been upgraded in 2004 at a cost of $17 million. New Viva Vision shows are created each year and are sequenced with around 15 pevious productions. Shows have included tributes to Queen, Kiss, and Don McLean's classic single "American Pie." Shown here is Summer of '69: Vegas or Bust.*

Binion's
GAMBLING
Take Your

Left: *Benny Binion made a legend of himself in Texas before moving out (or, more accurately, getting run out of town) and ending up in Las Vegas—where he disproved F. Scott Fitzgerald's belief that "there are no second acts in American lives." Born in 1904, Binion was raised by horse traders, gamblers, roughnecks, oilmen, cowboys, and other characters out of Texas dreams. During the Roaring Twenties, Binion ran illegal craps and lottery games, did some bootlegging, and carried two .45s and a .38. These guns weren't a flamboyant affectation. Binion was tried for two shootings—both were judged to be self-defense—and was suspected in several other killings. According to A. D. Hopkins in his article "The Cowboy Who Pushed the Limits" for* the Las Vegas Review Journal, *by the early 1950s, Dallas had enough of Benny Binion and vice versa, so Binion took his act to Las Vegas and made significant changes in gambling that still resonate today. Binion opened the Horseshoe and did things differently: He raised the maximum craps bet to $500, was the first to put carpets on the floor, and used limousines to pick up guests at the airport. Binion's Horseshoe was the first to offer free drinks to slot players. According to Leo Lewis, who worked for Binion's and many other Vegas casinos, "(Binion) said, 'If you wanta get rich, make little people feel like big people.'" Binion went to prison for tax evasion in the 1950s, and the Binion family lost control of the Horseshoe until the 1960s. Binion's sons, Jack and Ted, had their own ideas about running casinos and one of them was to take over the World Series of Poker from the Riverside Casino in Reno and blow up that card tournament into the multimillion-dollar spectacle it is today.*

Righ: *The Hand of Faith is one of the many wonders you will encounter by stepping off Fremont Street and into the Golden Nugget. The world's largest gold nugget on public display, the Hand of Faith is 875 troy ounces (sixty pounds), for all the world to see just by stepping inside. The Golden Nugget has proudly proclaimed its 1905 vintage since 1946, when it was the sixth casino built downtown, and the first to be constructed from the ground up as a casino. According to the PBS film* Las Vegas: An Unconventional History, *the man who built the Golden Nugget, Guy McAfee, was as classic a character as Las Vegas has ever produced. During the 1920s and 1930s, McAfee was the commander of the Los Angeles Police Department's vice squad even as he ran saloons and brothels and illegal gambling dens all around town—while his wife was a Hollywood madam. In the late 1930s, Judge Fletcher Bowron was elected mayor of Los Angeles as a reformer. Those reforms swept McAfee to Las Vegas, where gambling, brothels, quickie divorces, and other vices and immoralities were institutions. McAfee bought the Pair-O-Dice Club on Highway 91 and renamed it the 91 Club. He delayed the opening to coincide with the very public Las Vegas divorce of Clark Gable and Ria Langham Clark in 1939. McAfee liked taxes about as much as he liked laws, so he formed the town of Paradise as a tax shelter for the 91 Club and other hotels, clubs, and casinos along Highway 91. McAfee left Los Angeles with the law on his tail, but his homesickness inspired him to call Highway 91 "the Strip" in honor of the Sunset Strip in L.A. McAfee is regarded as one of the men who furthered the influence of gambling and casinos in the 1940s and 1950s, up until his death in 1960.*

EN NUGGET
GOLDEN
GOLDEN

B
Binion's
Take Your Picture With
$1,000,000

Left: *Fremont Street was an admirable effort by the City of Las Vegas to respect its own history and the casinos and personalities that made it famous. It was also a very expensive gamble that went against the usual thinking of casinos, that everything should be designed to keep people inside, with their heads down over the slot machines and the gaming tables. But Fremont Street was a $70 million gamble that worked. By March 1996, gaming revenues for the downtown casinos had jumped 16 percent.*

Right: *What was Sassy Sally is now Vegas Vicky and what was Sassy Sally's slots parlor is now Girls of Glitter Gulch, a topless joint that makes the lights of Fremont Street glow a little redder. Girls of Glitter Gulch is a throwback to the time when blocks 16 and 17 were the place to take a walk on the wild side.*

Plaza
GOLDEN GATE
LAS VEGA
Get up to $125 In Comps
BEST TAIL IN TOWN!
FRESH HOT POPCORN

Right: *A supersized blue martini and nouveau-retro Vegas sign welcome one and all to the Fremont East District. Anchored by the El Cortez Hotel, Fremont East is three blocks of vintage Las Vegas bars, restaurants, and hotel/casinos made accessible by a $5 million improvement project in 2007. What you'll find on Fremont East is true to the signs: a nouveau-retro Las Vegas experience.*

Left: *Looking northwest out of the Fremont Street Experience toward Main Street. The Plaza Hotel was originally called the Union Plaza in honor of the Union Pacific Railroad, which ran the City of Los Angeles train service from Chicago to Los Angeles, by way of Las Vegas, from 1936 to 1971. The Union Plaza opened in 1971, and it was the first hotel/casino that train passengers saw when they stepped into the station. The City of Los Angeles service phased out in 1971, when Amtrak took over long-distance passenger train operations in the United States. Amtrak renamed the train that ran through Las Vegas the Desert Wind in 1979, and service into Las Vegas continued until May 1997, when budget cuts forced them to drop service through Las Vegas. The Union Plaza became the Plaza in the middle of all this, and while Las Vegas no longer has passenger train service, the Greyhound and Amtrak bus services stop at the Plaza. There has long been talk of a high-speed Desert Xpress train running from Victorville, California, to Las Vegas, which would cover the 190 miles in just over an hour—at a cost of nearly $4 billion.*

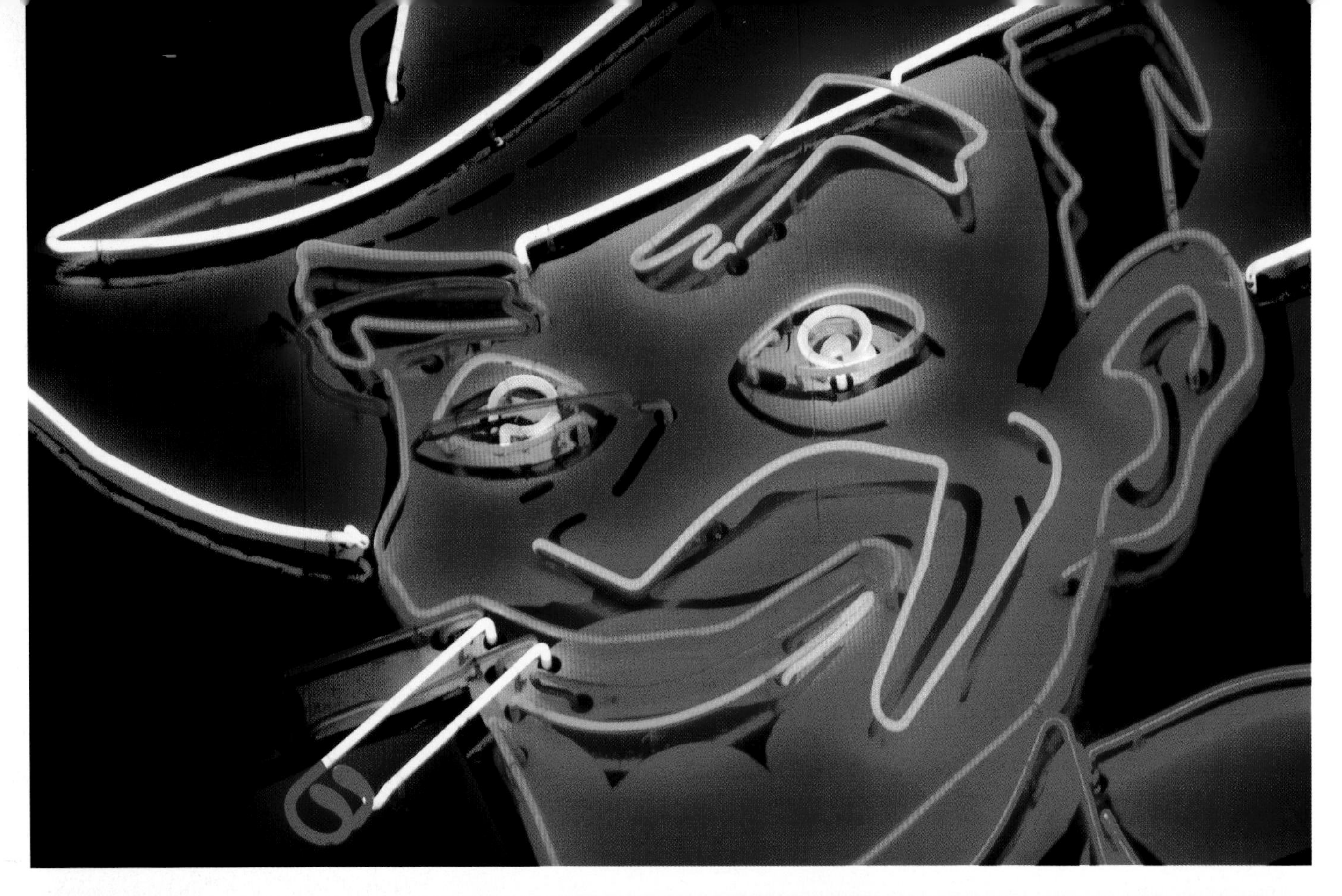

Left: *Vegas Vic went up with the Pioneer Hotel in 1951, and for many years the electric cowboy was the best-known symbol of Las Vegas. Originally, Vegas Vic was a forty-foot-tall neon statue with a waving arm who would say "Howdy, pardner!" every fifteen minutes. According to legend—and the book* Weird Las Vegas and Nevada*—Lee Marvin was in Las Vegas in 1966 to shoot the movie* The Professionals*. The cast and crew were staying at the Mint, directly across from the talking sign. "Howdy, pardner!" every fifteen minutes was too much of a welcome, prompting someone to fire metal-tipped arrows and maybe even bullets into the sign. Lee Marvin may or may not have actually done the deed, but he gladly took credit for it, and Vegas Vic was silenced. Vic started talking again in the 1980s, and managed to say "I do" when he made Sassy Sally an honest woman. But now he is silent again, drowned out by the sound and fury of the Fremont Street Experience.*

Left: *Crocodile rock—or jazz, anyway. A detail of the bottom of the main sign at the Orleans casino.*

Above: *This purty little gal is Sassy Sally. At one time, Sassy Sally's was a burlesque club called Reed's Cabaret, but when that fell out of fashion, it turned into Sassy Sally's slots casino. The Sassy Sally and Vegas Vic neon signs were "married" during the construction of the Fremont Street Experience. Marriage is always transformative, and Sassy Sally became Vegas Vicky while Vic lost a bit off the top of his hat in order to fit under the canopy. The Pioneer Club is now a gift shop and Sassy Sally's has been transformed into a topless club called Girls of Glitter Gulch.*

Right: *According to Erin Stellmon at the Neon Museum, this neon sign "is known as 'The Dancing Girl,' which is part of Fremont Street East's collection of installed signs and not a part of the Neon Museum."*

Hard Rock
CAFE
CVS
RAINBOW BAR & GRILL
WIDE SHOES
CVS

Left: *There was a time when all the showgirls, revues, nightclub singers, comedians, big bands, and other Vegas entertainments were all just a giant shill to lure people into the casinos—where the real money was. The entertainment side of Las Vegas has evolved over the years away from a lure to a central attraction. Las Vegas doesn't call itself "the Gambling Capital of the World," it calls itself "the Entertainment Capital of the World." The Hard Rock Hotel and Casino opened in 1995 and flooded the entire building with music: there are lyrics on all the walls, a corridor of rock 'n' roll photographs, and the slot machines are themed by songs and bands. The Hard Rock is rock 'n' roll 24-7 and some of it is live, coming from their venue, known as the Joint. Going against the "more is more" mores of Las Vegas, the Joint opened as a 300-person venue, which attracted bands like the Sex Pistols, who didn't mind playing in a small, smoky room. The Hard Rock is located off the Strip, but is thriving as the young crowds flock to a rock 'n' roll Kaaba. The place is loud, there are girls dancing on poles, and it is loaded with pretty young people. In 2008 the Joint was remodeled as part of a $750 million expansion of the Hard Rock. The size of the room was doubled but it was kept intimate through standard Las Vegas magic. If the owners hoped the new room would attract talent, they were satisfied, as April 2009 saw Carlos Santana sign up for an extended run, and that same month featured the Killers and Paul McCartney—a mixture of modern and classic that is going to fuel the Hard Rock Café as one of Las Vegas's best music venues.*

Right: *H is for Hard Rock, but also for Hooters and the Harley-Davidson Café. The Harley-Davidson Café is a motorcycle museum in a restaurant, a place to rinse the sand and bugs out of your teeth from a hard ride in the desert and fill your jangled stomach with solid American food: steaks, hamburgers, and Southwestern barbecue. The place is loaded with motorcycles—on the floor, on conveyor belts, in photos, videos, everywhere: vintage and modern, motorcycles ridden by movie outlaws and motorcycles ridden by celebrities, with a special tribute to Ann-Margaret, plus the 1953 Special Flat Tracker Racer that she used in her Las Vegas show. The Harley-Davidson Café also has the world's heaviest flag, a seven-ton version of the Stars and Stripes made out of 44,000 chain links. Harley-Davidson is an all-American brand in an all-American city.*

HUNT'S
STRAND
OPEN LANES
DANCE
Hunick's
GAMBLING MUSEUM & STOR
Perry's
SUPPER CLUB
LIQUOR
STORE

Left: *Neon signs from Las Vegas and all over decorate an elevator shaft in the middle of Neonopolis. Opened in May 2002 to great fanfare and greater hopes, the 250,000-square-foot retail and entertainment complex cost $100 million to rehabilitate. Neonopolis struggled to find itself at first, with tenants moving in and out while all of Las Vegas watched the complex struggle like a newborn doe. But the Southern Nevada Museum of Fine Art moved here in September 2008, and now with Las Vegas Telemundo taking up office space and Star Trek: The Experience moving from the Las Vegas Hilton, Neonopolis is becoming the new town square for downtown.*

Above: *The Neon Boneyard (not Graveyard) is a part of the Neon Museum, established in 1996 to preserve Las Vegas history. The Neon Museum rescued these signs from the backlot of the Young Electric Sign Company and keeps them exposed but relatively safe in two dirt lots along Las Vegas Boulevard, about a mile north of Fremont Street. A tour of the Neon Boneyard will get you up close and personal with signs that once shone proudly over the Stardust, Fitzgeralds, the Aladdin, the Landmark, the Silver Slipper, and also more obscure places from Las Vegas's past, like the Castaways, the Debbie Reynolds Hotel and Casino, and the El Portal. The Neon Museum is hoping to turn the Neon Boneyard into a museum, where Las Vegas's past is carefully restored as the ongoing redevelopment of Las Vegas casts out the old and replaces it with the new.*

Left: *Lucky the Clown has been pointing the way to Circus Circus since 1976, when YESCO installed the 126-foot, eighty-four-ton pylon sign.*

Below left: *The Sahara gave its name to Sahara Avenue, which marks the northern end of the Strip. The Sahara pylon sign was remade and installed in 1996, but the classic look of 1950s Las Vegas is still there, the first or last thing you see on the Strip.*

Below right: *In continuous operation for forty years, The World Famous Chapel of the Bells on Las Vegas Boulevard aptly demonstrates the principal that lurid neon can be used for love and money.*

Right: *"Drive carefully" and "Come back soon"—these messages were displayed on the back of the original "Welcome to Fabulous Las Vegas" sign in 1959, and they are still true today. By the time the twenty-first century rolled around, forty million visitors were coming to Las Vegas each year by private and passenger jets, buses, cars, bicycles, and the seat of their pants. Given Las Vegas's ability to lure people by means of popular entertainment, innovative luxuries, and exciting experiences, that number doesn't look to stop growing anytime soon.*

DRIVE
CAREFULLY
Come Back
SOON

PICTURE CREDITS

All photos by Jason Hawkes and Karl Mondon, with the exception of:
Pages 8, 9, 10, 11, 12, 15, 16, 32, 52, 53, 65, 82, 83, 86 right, 87, 102, 116, 126 right, and 143, courtesy of Corbis.
Pages 86 left, 110, 111, 112, and 140, courtesy of Anova Image Library/Barrett Adams.
Page 27 courtesy of Getty Images.

Project Editor: Frank Hopkinson
Designer: Cara Rodgers
Art Director: John Heritage
Editor: David Salmo
Production: Oliver Jeffreys

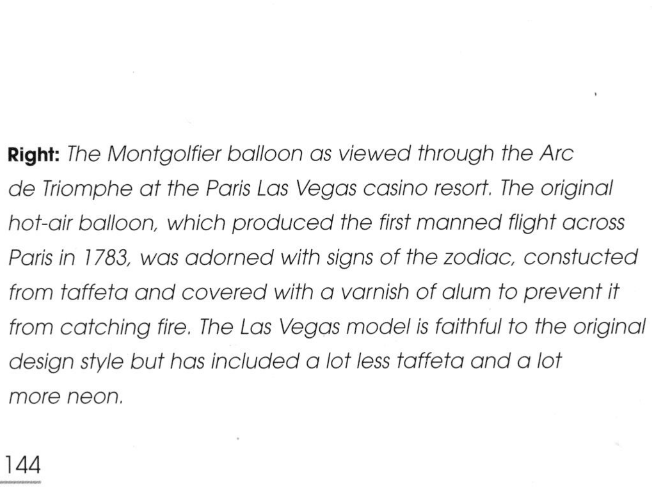

Right: *The Montgolfier balloon as viewed through the Arc de Triomphe at the Paris Las Vegas casino resort. The original hot-air balloon, which produced the first manned flight across Paris in 1783, was adorned with signs of the zodiac, constucted from taffeta and covered with a varnish of alum to prevent it from catching fire. The Las Vegas model is faithful to the original design style but has included a lot less taffeta and a lot more neon.*